GAṄGĀ AS DIVINE ORIGIN

GAṄGĀ AS DIVINE ORIGIN

Dr. Kamal Shankar Srivastava

AGAM KALA PRAKASHAN
DELHI

First Published 2022

ISBN: 978-81-950098-0-0

Published by:
For **Agam Kala Prakashan**
34, Central Market, Ashok Vihar
Delhi - 110 052
Tel.: 91-11-27212195, 43513480
Fax: 91-11-27212195
Email: agamkala101@gmail.com, agambook@yahoo.com
www.agamkala.in

Composed by:
Sushil Kumar
Delhi - 110 052
Mobile: 9891395309

Printed in India.

CONTENTS

PREFACE

From the snow Ganges origin high in the Himalayas, this sacred river flows through the holy cities and the great plain of Northern India to the Bay of Bengal. The life giving water of the Ganges have assumed legendary powers in the form of the Hindu goddess Gaṅgā, the source of creation and abound once. In fact the mysterious Gaṅgā is the essence of the divine mother bringing increase and salvation, but also death and destruction. Indeed there is not a river anywhere in the world which has not something of beauty and mystery. According to Dr. A.L. Basham, no river is endowed with these qualities in such full measure as the Gaṅgā. It is not in the best surprising that ancient Indian thought of the Gaṅgā as sacred, a goddess in her own right, descending from the head of the great god Śiva himself. The Gaṅgā which is also called Alakanaṅdā or Dyundhuni or Dyunadi is mentioned in the Ṛgveda and in satapatha Brāhmaṇa. It is also mentioned in Patanjali Mahābhāṣya and also in the Brahmanḍa purāṇa as well in Kālidāsa's Raghuvaṃśa. Gaṅgā is also known as Bhāgirathī and Jāhṇavī. The Yoginī tantra refers to it. The victory of the Gaṅgā represents the furthest extent of the Kurū rule. The Gaṅgā the most sacred river of the Hindus, is formed by the conjunction of two sister streams, named Bhāgirathī and Alkanaṅdā. The Bhāgirathī rises from the Gaṇgotrī glacier at Gaumukh - an ice-cave, in the Uttarkashi district of modern Uttaranchal state. After cutting through the narrow gorges of lower Himalaya. Bhāgirathī joins the Alkanandā which emerges from satopanta glacier above Badrināth and the combined river assumes the name of Gaṅgā. It enters the plains at Haridwar. The Gaṅgā turns its directions from north west to southeast and then flows majestically in the east from about 1200 km, passing through the plains of Uttaranchal, Uttar Pradesh, Bihar and Bengal before discharging its water into the Bay of Bengal through the numerous mouths of its great delta of the many Himalayas tributaries of the Gaṅgā which join it on its left bank, may be mentioned the names of Rāmgaṅgā, Gomatī, Sarayū, Ghagharā, Rāptī Ganḍak, Koṣī and Mahanaṅdā. According to the Markanḍeya Purāṇa the Gaṇges is described as Tṛipathagāminī in having three courses. According to Harivamsa King Purrāṇa lived with Urvaśī for five years on the bank of the rivers Mandākānī which is another name of the Ganges. Gaṅgā is the name of a river. This river is called Mandākinī which descends from the sky with all the fairy of rushing water and which is borne by the God Śiva on one of his matted locks. Numerous Rgvedic descriptions of Saraswatī river are later applied to Gaṅgā. Sataswati's home is in heaven. She fills the realms of the earth, and wide trust, the firmament. The worshippers hopes that the river will descend from heaven and from the mountain hear his prayers. It is observed the signification of Gaṅgā's descent from heaven and the prevalence of the theme is art and myth. In later literature. Gaṅgā is described as the path of human a river flowing through the sky. We may recall her home among the stars in the realm of Viṣṇupāda, the path of Viṣṇu between Urśa major and the Pole star.

Several legends describe Gaṅgā as originating from a tree. On their journey north to mount Kailāśa. The five pāṅḍava brothers heroes of the Mahābhārata - came upon the hermitage of Nara and Nārāyaṇa (This is form of Viṣṇu) filled with celestial trees and flowers; And they build the rounded trunk of a great jungle tree. It is fresh and shining and the hard by the gigantic jungle tree, the Bhāgirathī of graceful descent with stairs of rulers and corals.

The Sarasvatī river is described as issuing from the water jug or kamaṇḍala of God Brahmā, then staring on its downward course at the fountain of Palāsh, it passes through Kedāra. It is sun, one of the three most famous sources of Gaṅgā like Sarasvatī, Gaṅgā also issues from a Kamandala.

Gaṅgā is need one with Soma (The immortal drink that fell from the Kumbha at Prayāg) which the feminine qualities and all the life giving liquifies including Semen, with themom, the lotus and serpents. By contrast the force of Agni the sun bird of Viṣṇu. At the some time Indian thought in its careless effort to achieve a unitary pimple states water is female and tira is male life is from of their intercourse. The conjunction as we see under it's the relation between Gaṅgā and Śiva in the figurative of the Hindu Temples.

By the time of *Mahābhārata* (C 400BC - 400 AD), Brāhmaṇ and Saṃsāra have became fundamental to Indian thought. Alongwith them grew up several other ideas then reinforced a single source of generation. One of these is Śakti. The property in a substance that produces an effect. It is stogic logas, the power in the deity enabling him to produce diverse shapes from his own essence. As a non-Aryan perception. It has probably existed in India since the beginning and was slowly brought into the vedic texts. We first perceive it in the power of Agni, dwelling in the earth, in the plants in the water. He is in the stores and within men. He lives in cattle in the horse with the fading of the Aryan vision. Śakti is transformed into a feminine principle, becoming a goddess. Eventually this Śakti Combines with Māyā the belief that all forms are but an infusion of the formless. The present ventujre entitled "Gaṅgā as divine origin is a modest attempt of compile a concise detection in Indian art under review by making liberal and simple legendary and intensive researches done by all those Savants, archaeologists art historian and Ideologist especially Art-historian Dr. A. K. Coomaraswamy, Dr C. Sirvaramamurti, Dr. Stella Kramrisch. Iconographist Dr. J.N. Banerjea, Dr. Vasudeva S. Agarwala. The significance of Gaṅgā as sacred and religious views, it has a unique place in the Hindu culture and civilization as per India is concerned. It is impact rediscovered reviewed and systematically explored and mentioned properly.

In the last but not the least, Smt. Sangeeta Srivastava & both of my sons, Sri Rishabh Kamal and Sri Tushit Kamal it is for their unfailing cooperation and to share their time to carve the monograph. I am much indebted to Sri Sanjay Kumar Dey for computerized manuscript for the present monogram and serially arranging the photographs.

I am highly obliged for late Dr. Agam Prasad, M/s Agam Kala Prakashan, New Delhi, proprietor Smt. Lila Devi & Shri A.K. Pandey, Manager; Kedarnath to accept the same and for their keen interest to publish the manuscript in the present form.

(Vijaya Daśamī) **Kamal S. Srivastava**
Dated: 15th October 2021

LIST OF PLATES

1. Brahmā pouring water on Viṣṇu's food, Hoysala, 12th century A.D., Nuggihajji, Mysore.
2. Brahmā pouring water on Viṣṇu's foot, Western Cālukya, 12th century A.D., Hampi, Mysore.
3. Umāsaṃhitā Śiva receiving Gaṅgā on his locks, approaching in Gaṅgāvataraṇa, karaṇa, 10th century A.D., Nepal.
4. Gaṅgādhara, close-up, suggesting the receiving of Gaṅgā on his locks by Śiva. Early Çola, 9th century A.D. Koyambatur, Tamil Nadu.
5. Gaṅgā as cāmaradhārinī, along with Gaurī, for Naṭarāja dancing on bull. Pāla, 11th century A.D. Saṇkarbandha, Bangladesh.
6. Gaṅgā approaching Śiva as a bride, Gupta, 5th century A.D., Rajouna, Bihar.
7. Gaṅgādhara appeasing Pārvatī, while receiving Gaṅgā on his locks. Early Çola, 11th century A.D. Gaṅgāikonḍācolapuram, Tamil Nadu.
8. Gaṅgādhara with Pārvatī vexed with her face turned away. Early Çola, 11th century A.D. Mayuram, Tamil Nadu.
9. Gaṅgā as an umbrella or cauri or canopy above Śiva, Pallava, 7th century A.D. Kāncīpuram, Tamil Nadu, National Museum, New Delhi.

CHAPTER 1

INTRODUCTION

1. THE ORIGIN AND SOURCES

The divine origin of *Gaṅgā* from Kamanḍal of Lord Brahmā to the hair of Jaṭā of Lord Śiva and thus beyond high Himalayas in the vast reaches of the Tibetan plateau, likes Mount Kailāśa. In the Indian tradition, it holds the same meaning as Śaivitas for Hinduism. As such it seems less a place than a state of mind, constellated with the dream and aspirations of a thousand pilgrims who shall never make the journey except in their hearts. But Kailāśa is a place, a shimmering mountain of twenty thousand feet. In some of the ancient writings - *Hindu, Buddhist*, even Chinese and Tibetan - *Kailua* is also the home of Gaṅgā, which flows from its slopes, dividing into four streams, to grace the world of men.

Near the foot of *Kailua* lies *Mānasarovar*, the Lake of the Mind (*sarovar*, in Sanskrit, signifying lake: *manas*, mind or thought), an other supposed source of *Gaṅgā*. Like the great mountain, it has been a center of pilgrimage since the early centuries of the Christian era, famous among *Hindus* and among *Buddhists* of all the northern countries. *Tibet, China, Japan.* At fifteen thousand feet, the ice-blue water covers an area of two hundred square miles, its regularly indented shore set in a cluster of mountains that rise abruptly from the endless expense of plains.

In the figukrative geography of the *Purāṇas*, Indian religious texts from the eight centuries of our era, we confront the image of Asia as a four-sided lotus, each petal containing one of thegreat regions: China to the east, Persia to the west, India to the south, and, to the north, the obscure realms of Turkestan.[1] And out of *Mānasarovar*, the Lake of the Mind, went a river in each direction to water the land. Within India itself, the four great rivers of the north *Gaṅgā, Yamunā*, the *Indus*, and the *Brahmaputra* - all take rise in the *Himalayas* and were thought of as flowing from *Mānasarovar*, which is reality lies slightly to their north. But this was not known until the early nineteenth century.

The *Gaṇges* itself is born several hundred miles south of *Kailua* in the *Gangotrī* glacier, a mountain of ice nearly twenty miles long and three miles wide, surrounded by peaks twenty - one thousand to twenty - four thousand feet high. From here its two main sources - the *Alakanandā* and the *Bhāgirathī* - flow past the sacred villages of *Badrīnāth* and *Gangotrī*, long since regarded as the most revered centers of pilgrimage. The journey from *Rishikesh*, nearly two hunded miles south, once lay across dirt tracks and over precarious bridges that swayed violently in the wind. These bridges, called *jhūlās*, which still exist in remote places, are made from two pieces of twisted rope strung between the chiffs. Smaller ropes hand down, supporting short pieces of wood at right angles to the railings. Across these strips areplaced lengths of split *bamboo* that provide the actual walkway.[2] The track is seldom more than ren inches wide. Since the

---

1 In Egyptian religious art, a lotus flower is used as a symbol for the remote mountains of the upper *Nile*, which concealed the source of the river.

2 *Albereuni*, the Muslim historian who visited India in the eleventh century, gives a traveler's report of a river "which is everal times crossed on bridges consisting of planks tied with cords to two canes which stretch from rock to rock, and ar fastered to milestones constructed on either side. People carry

1940s, the Indian government has developed long stretches of the road, but the last few miles to Gangotrī are still done on foot.

Badrīnath is ancient and first appears in the *Mabābhārata*, the great Indian epic often compared with the *Iliad.* Though composed between 400 B.C. and A.D. 400, it describes real and mythological events that return to the beginnings of Indian civilization. It is said the *Manu* - the first man - built an ark at the time of the deluge. Eventually it settled on a peak at *Badrīnath*, where Manu recreated the human race. By his eponymous role as well as certain linguistic affinities. Manu is related to *Adam* and to *Minos*, the legendary king of Crete. India's greatest poet, *Kalidāsa*, who lived in thefifth century A.D., describes the mythical Himalayan city of *Alaka*, perhaps a shortened form of Alkanaṅdā:

Where maidens, who the gods would gladly wed
are fanned by breezes col with Gaṅgā's foam
in the shadows that the trees of heaven spread.

The town of Badrināth lies on the western bank of the *Alkanaṅdā* in a mile-wide valley set between the ridges of *Nar* and *Nārāyaṇa*, the somber rock catchdrals of *Viṣṇu* that rise to 19,500 feet, "higher than the flight of eagles," and behind them Nilakantha Peak, a dazzling *pyramid of snow* touching 21,600.

The source of the river descends from *Vasudhārā* Falls, seven or eight miles beyond the town, and can be reached by following a route long used by merchants and pilgrims traveling to and from Tibet. Starting from *Badrināth*, the road runs north along the Alkanaṅda, then across a broad rocky plain to the tiny village of *Mana*, where it branches, one track leading to the Mana Pass at eighteen thousand feet and on to *Mānasarovar*, 238 miles away, the other following the river to Vasudhārā. Pilgrims follow the 2½ mile track from Mana to immerse themselves for a moment in theicy waters of the

---

the burdens on their shoulders over such a bridge, whilst below, at a depth of a hundred yards, the water foams as white as snow, threatening to shatter the rocks" See Alberuni, Alberuni's India trans. E. C. Sachau, Delhi, 1964, vol. I, p. 201.

falls where *Gaṅgā* is born. It is a place of beginnings; for in Indian tradition,water - as a substance without shape - reminds us of the potential (*pralaya*) that all things have before they assume name and form, before they become unalterable. At Vasudhara the stream is sometimes cut off by the fierce winds that blkow through the gorge. The natives regard this as a sign tha someone of evil temperament has come to absolve himself by rouching the source.

The village of Mana is like a hundred other *Himālayan* settlements:; tiny stone houses cling to the mountainside; along the terraces and in unlikely places grow stand of wheat, corn, and other vegetables. Its inhabitants are *Bhoṭiyās*, a Tibetan people found along the mountains as far as *Sikkim* and *Darjeeling*. Their name are short and powerful, the women full-bodied, with rich Mongolian faces and an openness that comes from working the fields and drending sheep. The few archaeological remains from the village include several carved figures of *lāmās* and an early *Brāhmī* script that dare to the sixth century A.D.

Through hidden tracks among the mountains, the people of *Mana* carry on a considerable trade with the little - known kingdom of *Bhutan*. Toward are end of July, when the snows have melted and the passes are clear, they set off in groups of a hundred or so with merchandise, chiefly grain, carried by sheep or goats. The entire affair takes about a month; ten days each way plus time for rest and provisioning - and the endless subtleties of buying and selling, sitting in the marketplace sipping tea and talking of clouds and weather, flocks and grain, and intimations of trhe world beyond that drift down through the mountains like a wayward snowflake in September.

As for Badrināth, its heart is the temple, a small stone building covered with a copper-plated roof and surmounted by a gilded ball. According to tradition, it was first established in the eighth century by the famous philosopher *Śankara*, though it has been destroyed a hundred times by icefalls rushing down from *Nārāyaṇa Parvat*. The statute may be older yet. For though it is worshipped as an image of *Viṣṇu*, there is every reason to believe it was originally meant to portray the *Buddha*,[3] at a time when the Himalayas were subject to strong Buddhist influence, especially under the Tibetan king *Srong-tsang-Gampo* (A.D. 629-647). Half concealed in the violet shadows of the sanctum, the black stone figure sits with legs crossed. One hand is raised, the palm facing outward in a gesture of benediction, the other resting in its lap, a pose typical of the *Buddha*. Another indication of its Buddhist affinities is the regular gifts sent to the temple by the *Tholing lamasery* in Tibet, from an unknown time in the past up untilk the border closing in the 1950s.

The chief priest is a *Numbudiri Brāhman* from Kerala, on the southwest coast of India, the original home of *Śankara*, and the contact has been maintained for over a thousand years. Near the temple is *Tapta Kuṇḍ*, a hot spring that serves the appurrenances of pilgrimage. Throughout the year, even with snow eoverieng the ground, it discharges boiling water that may be channeled to huts and private homes, providing a semblance of warmth. But except for thesummer months - from May to November - the temple is closed, and mostresidents descend to villages at lower attitudes. Besides a handful of *sādhus* and *sannyāsins* (holy men), there are few indications of life. Swami Tapovan, a saint of the Himalayas describes the scene at the height of winter; "No bird stirs; no animal moves about . . . . Even as the face is seen reflected in a mirror, the Soul perceives itself in the stillness of Nature.[4] The remple service itself is austere; the chanting of a short litany and then bathing in the spting. For widows and orphans, there is shaving of the head, a custom practiced during the *great Mela* (bathing fair) at Allahabad, where three rivers meet and the true devotee steps beyond time.

Further South the *Alkanaṅdā* River is joined by the *Mandākinī*, a lesser source that rises near *Kedārnāth*, another center of pilgrimage.

---

3 *Kanti Nautriyal*, The Archaeology of the Kumaon (Varanasi, 1969), p. 153 and also Swami Maharaj Tapovan, *Iśwara Darshan* (Madras, 1969) p. 153.

4 Darian, Steven G. Delhi (Reprint) Delhi 2001 pp 7-8 The *Gaṅgā* in Myth and History.

The shrine at *Kedar* is set on a broad treeless plain studded with glacial lakes. Certain architectural features as well as several of the sculptural panels devoted to *Śiva* all date from the tenth of eleventh century, while other characteristics seem as late as the sixteenth. The river itself flows from *Kedār* Peak, which looms above the temple at a height of twenty-one thousand feet. During the months of travel - in May and September - the entire route is thick with pilgrims, who come by foot and by bus, young and old, men and women, the rich and the penniless, the aged and the infirm, driven at times by something less than faith but more than curiosity. For, despite the occasional inns offering simple meals and shelter, it is not an easy journey.

At *Deoprayag*, the Alkananda joins the Bhāgirathī, the other main source of Gaṅgā, which rises beyond the pilgrimage center of *Gangotrī*. The route to Gangotrī follows steep mountainsides along the Bhagīrathī Valley, passing among dense forests of cedar and pine and through little towns all with a curious sameness about them. The approach is through a rocky defile that booms with the sound of the river. Considering its age, the town seems almost makeshift. Apart from pilgrims, the only inhabitants are priests, *yogīs*, and a few shopkeepers. In the surrounding caves, sannyasins often spend their last days in meditation before embracing the mystery. From November to May, everything is closed. Only a few ascertics stay on, sustaining themselves one way or another. Besides the temple, most structures are built from wood and tin, though the cedar, if properly cured, can last for centuries. The temple itself is made of stone and dedicated to *Bhagīrathā*, whose name is intimately connected with the birth of Gaṅgā. Inside there is a small statue of the river goddess with her companions the rivers *Yamunā* and Sarasvatī.

But the true source of *Gaṅgā* is at *Gomukh* (13,500 feet), the giant ice cave fourteen miles beyond the town. The journey is difficult; but the site, strange and compelling, says all that can be said about beginnigs. No fixed road leads from Gangotrī; only modest stone cairns guide the traveller. Clay pillars three hundred feet high cling precariously to the enclosing walls of the valley. Gradually the land levels to a bouolder-covered plain nearly a mile long, sloping always upward toward the thick pine forest of *Chirbāsā*. Heere, at 11,800 feet, lies the only habitation along the way, a large pilgrim shelter (*dharmashālā*) that accommodates forty or fifty people. The pines of Chirbāsā have aqchieved a sanctity all their own. Even the poet *Kālidāsa* speaks of *Gaṅgā* flowing toward the pines along the high peaks of *Himālaya*. From Chirbāsā it is another six miles, and most pilgrims set off at dawn, dompel the full circle by nightfall. The last few miles run through stand of birch trees the recede near the perpetual snow line,[5] and the only things remaining are wizened shrubs and the yellow Brahmā lotus that smells with the sweetness of the sun.

The ice cave-facing onto a tiny pool-rises over two hundred feet beneath its; granite shell, and standing just above it is the peak of *Śivalinga* (19,630 feet), golden gray, the color of sea relics. For this is *Gomukh*, source of all begotten things, where shadows struggle into form "against the white unending canvass of eternity," where all that has ever been exists unuttered. Besides the occasional pilgrim, there are only shepherds pasturing their sheep along the small uland valleys. Men of incredible endurance, they often camp out on the plains-at thirteen thousand feet - without tents or firewood.

The shape of the cave forms a natural amphitheatre that catches distant sounds: the shifting of ice, frost shattering on high peaks. At night the wind runs stronger; the entire atmosphere hums with the susurrous discourse of *yakshas* and *gandharvas*, divine beings believed to inhabit remote places that humans never see. Ordinarily such a scene might be terrifying, except that one can never think of death at Gomukh.

From here and *Badrināth*, the great sources descend to the *sangam* (the confluence) at *Deoprayag*, where they become the Ganges, the River of India. Flowng south, it passes through *Rishikesh*,

5 Bitch bark is strong yet malleable and since early times has been used as a form of clothing by ascertics living in the forests.

the last point in the *Himālayas* before *Gaṅgā* enters the plains. Unlike many other religious centers, Rishikesh is not mentioned in early literature and the town itself speaks nothing of antiquity. Here the sacred and profane are formally divided by the river. On one side: the endless rows of simple houses, workmen's sheds, and piles of dismembered auto parts. On theother: the *ashrams*, the centers of learning, and in thenearby hills the caves of holy men. Aside from a footbridge at the far end and a power launch tht runs every half hour from dawn to sunset, nothing connects the two worlds but the agreement that the town is a holy place.

At the point where *Gaṅgā* enters the plains, breaking out between the hills, lies Hardwar, the Gate of *Viṣṇu* (*Hari*, a name of *Viṣṇu*; dvara, the Sanskrit word for door or gate). The pilgrims gather here - in May and September - provisioning for the long journey north. At all times, the shops are filled with emollients for the spiritual traveler: tins of food, coarse coal-brown handwoven blankets, modest camp stoves, pots and cooking utensils, no two exactly the same, and brass tipped walking sticks stained black. Everywhere too are earthen pots, often in pairs and joined with a bamboo pole. For here and at *Rishikesh, Gaṅgā* water is considered its holiest. People come from all over the country-servants, pilgrims - to fill the pots and take them home for special occasions such as marriage or death or other times when *Gaṅgā* is called upon to remind them of the dreams that have faded from their hearts. It is an old custom. *Abul Fazl*, a sixteenth century chronicler, records the habits of the great *Moghul* emperor *Akbar*: "His majesty calls this source of life the water of immortality . . . . Both at home and on his travels he drinks Gaṇges water. Trustworthy persons stationed on thebanks of the river dispatch the water in sealed jars . . . . Now that his majesty is in the Punjab, water is brought from *Hardwar*."[6]

6 *Abul Fazil*, *Ain-i-Akbari*, trans. H. Blochmannn (Delhi, 1871), vol. 1, p. 58. Even among Muslims the custom goes back at least to *Muhammed bin Tughluq* (1325-1351), Sultan of Delhi, See *Aziz Ahmd*, *Islamkic Culture* in the Indian Setting (Oxford, 1964), p. 177.

As a wedding drink at Hindu marriages, *Gaṇges* water was accorded the highest honor. We glimpse the custom from the dikary of *Jean Tavernier*, a French jeweler who visited India several times in the seventeenth century. *Gaṇges* water, he explains, "must be brought from a great distance by the *Brāhmins*, in earthen vessels glazed inside, which the Grand Brāhmin has placed his seal upon. This water is not given except at the end of the repast . . . for each of the guests three or four cupfuls are poured out and the more of it the bridgegroom gives . . . so is the esteemed the more generous and magnificent. As this water comes from so far and the Chief Brahmin charges a certain tax on each pot . . . there is sometimes 2,000 or 3,000 Rupees worth of it consumed at a wedding."[7]

The life of Hardwar revolves around the *ghāṭs*, the stone steps and causeways leading to the water. One may spend a day watching the endless coming and going of things: little troops of men from Delhi, Rajasthan, or towns without names, gathering pots of water for the journey of a thousand miles, this perhaps their only chance to visit Hardwar, the holy place, before they die. Then there are the bathers, some of whom rent small thatched one - room shelters at the water's edge, alternately immersing themselves and withdrawing into the huts, for hours on end. At sunset bells toll from the temples near the shore, and those with hopes or prayers launch tiny boats of leaves, filled with rose petals and a lighted candle. The shells gather slowly, forming a long line of tiny flames that moves tentatively but inclutably along the current, out into the great river that widens here to a mile. At times the line wobbles and disappears but always somewhere, further off, appears a tip of flame, a prayer that, one way or another, finds the sea.

Hardwar is an ancient town. Its name appears in different forms since the time of *Mahābhārata* over two thousand years ago. It has been known as Mokshadvāra (the Door of Freedom), *Māyāpurā* (the City of Illusion), and *Gaṅgādvāra* (the Gate of *Gaṅgā*), its

---

7 *Jean Baptiste Tavernier*, *Travels in India* (London, 1925), vol. 2. pp. 253-254.

most common name. Sculpture fragments, coins, and numerous foundations allude to its antiquity, but nothing visual remains. We glimpse it but briefly in the early literature. The seers sang hymns at *Gaṅgādvāra*, and several heroes of the *Mahābhārata -Bhīṣma* and *Arjuna* - do penance here at the point where *Gaṅgā* meets the plains.

Unlike many other ancient cities, *Hardwar* has escaped the anonymous embrace of time, perhaps because it never was a kingdom or a capital or a place where armies fought. It never threw up palaces or monuments, and so it remains what it has always been: a kingdom of the mind, frequented by pilgrims and travelers who gather wherever highways meet, where roads begin and end. In the seventh century A.D. the *Buddhist* pilgrim *Hiuen Tsiang* reached *Hardwar* after an incredible overland journey from China. He describes the town as roughly "twenty li [3 ½ miles] in circuit. The inhabitants are very numerous, and the pure streams of the river flow round on every side; it produces native copper . . . pure crystal, and precious vases. There are always hundreds and thousands of people gathered together here from distant quarters to bathe and wash in its waters.[8] In *Moghul* times, Hardwar remained an unimportant thoughnot forgottenoutpost. Under *Akbar* it was one of the twenty - eight towns where copper coins were produced: silver and gold were minted elsewhere, at more important centers.[9]

As we will see later, the image of *Gaṅgā* is intimarely connected with *Himalaya*. She is "the child of the mountain" in a very real sense. For it is during the summer months of March and April - when the plains grow hot and dry and dusty-that the snows melt on the high peaks and the river, fed by a thousand icy streams, carries its life - giving water to the parched earth and its inhabitants.[10]

Together *Gaṅgā* and *Śiva* Illustrate a primordial relationship prefigured in the *Vedas* and hinted at as early as the Indus civilization.

---

8 *Hiuen Tsiang*, Travels of Hiuen Tsiang, trans. *Samuel Beal* (Calcutta. 1957). Vol. 2, p. 226.

9 *Abdul Fazl,* vol. 1. p.32.

10 *Darian Steven*, G. Op cit. p. 13.

We have seen them together in myth and art. Ultimately their relationship underlies the spiritual architecture of the Hindu temple as it evolves from its primitive antecedents. For this reason, it is necessary to trace the development of the temple - and its exemplar the *Śiva shrine* - from the beginnings.

Gertrude Levy makes it abundantly clear that the earliest religious enclosures were the prehistoric mountain caves of northern Spain and southern France, which served as both *tombs* and *shrines*.[11] The inaccessibility of its sacred pictures suggests that the sanctum was not a polace for people to gather but a repository of potent forces designed to ensure the fortunes of the tribe. In this sense, it is closer to the *Hindu* temple than to the western *cathedral*.

The *Vedic* literature demonstrates the evolution from tomb to temple. The original burial place served the dead "as a house or as a *monument*.[12] The site was marked with a stone slab, a mound of earth, or both. "Over thee," says the priest in the final ritual, I place this piece of earth . . . . Here let the Fathers keep this pillar firm for thee, and there let *Yama* make thee an abiding place.[13] We need but recall "the tree where Yama drinks with the gods" to perceive a correspondence between the tree and the stone pillar. This correspondence was strengthened by the *indigenous* custom of planting a sapling over the *grave*.[14] The tree as cenotaph becomes a home of the departed spirit. In the *Mahābhārata* and the *Jātaka* stories, we read of mkalign spirigs who waid in trees for unsuspecting passersby. The mound of earth, with its contents, also duplicates in miniature the mountain cave. "Here I build this rampart for the living," sings the Vedic poet. "May they survive a hundred *autumns*, and may they bury Death beneath this mountain."[15] Thus the tree, the pillar, and the mountain all come to mark the center of the site.

11 *Davian Stevan* G., The Gaṇges in the myth and Delhi (Reprint) 2010 p. 97.

12 SB XIII 8.1.1.

13 RVX. 18.13.

14 Agrawala V.S., Ancient Indian Folk Cults, p. 137.

15 ṚVX 18.4.

The stone element serves botht as center and as circumference of the entire configuration. After constructing the funeral mound, the priest encloses it is a ring of stones, which is regarded as a *womb.*[16] It is not surprising that stone, the least perishable material, was first reserved for the dead. As *Siegfried Gidedion* observes its enduring qualities made it the ideal substance from which to build a perpetual resting place for th dead. It was the grave, in fact, that gave birth to the first stone architecture.

The *Vedic* fire alter - a more highly structured antecedent of the *Hindu* temple - combines the functions of *tomb* and *temple.* In the ceremony, a golden image of a man and a golden disk representing the sun are placed above a lotus leaf. The sacrificer then places the leaf at the bottom of the fire alter, "for the lotus leaf is a womb.[17] And we find the *lotus*, a distinctly non-Aryan vegetal symbol, giving rise to the sun, to humankind, to the entire universe. According to the scriptures, the *tomb* is fashioned after the fire alter: "For when a Sacrificer builds a fire alter he thereby constructs for himself a [new] body for that distant world; but that sacrifice is not complete until themaking of a tomb."[18] The fact is implicit in the ritual itself: the universe is created anew by sacrifice of the Great *Purusha* (the original inchoate being from which the world was fashioned and who later evolves into the impersonal *Brahman* substance): and man, the little *Purusha*, by identifying himself with the cosmic act, becomes reinregrated with the universe. The point in any such ritual, as anthropologist A.M. Hocart explains, "is to make one thing equivalent to another so that by acting on one you can act on another . . . . Without these equivalencies there would be no point in the ritual . . . . The participants are deliberately seeking to establish an identity between man and the ritual objects, between ritual objects and the world, and so between man and the world."[19]

---

16 SB XIII. 8.2.2.: VII.1.1.12.

17 SB VII. 4.1.7.

18 XIII. 8.1.7.

19 Brihadaranyaka Up. 6.4.2-3.

The relation between tomb, tree, and monument is equally apparent in the evolution of the stupa, which has the same origins as the Hindu temple. The earliest stupa mounds, which may date to pre-Mauryan times, reveal a post running vertically through the center of the structure as a representation of the Tree of Life.[20] The Vedic literature describes the structures of the ungodly (the easterners, the Asuras), who make their sepulchers round, while those who are godly make theirs four - comered.[21] The "Ungodly" refers to the indigenous people who had not accepted the Vedic ritual but followed the age-old enchoric patterns of the subcontinent. These patterns continued undiminished until the second century B.C., when they burst out in thefully developed form of the Buddhist stupa.

The little mountain - rock or pillar - was a numinous object throughout the ancient world. In the Near East and in Mycenaean religion, it is interchangeable with the sacred tree as a dwelling place of god.[22] It occurs in the Old Testament (Gen. 28) representing Yahweh: "And Jacob Rose up in the morning, and took the stone he had put for a pillow, and set up a pillar, and poured oil upon thetop of it . . . . 'And this stone, which I have set for a pillar, shall be God's house.'" The Vedas contain frequent references to the pillar or stambha as a cosmological principle, and various gods are identified with the power in it. Perhaps because of his column of fire: "And the Lord went before them in a pillar of fire" - the chief association falls to Agni, whose column of flame supports the vault of heaven.[23] In a long hymn, the early thinkers search for the god behind the symbol: "Who out of many, tell me, is that Stambha to whom the parhwayslead . . . to whom the Waters make their way with longing?[24]

---

20 Mbh XIII. 141.

21 Matsya P. XI. 20-21.

22 Eamanayya, p. 2.

23 *Dorian Steven* G. p. 99.

24 Mrs. Sinclair Stevenson, The Rites of the Twice - Born (London, 1920), p. 396.

Certain passages in the Vedas indicate the generative properties of the stambha. We read in a hymn to Agni: "He who knows the Golden Reed that stands in the sea, he is the Lord of Life." The Sanskrit word vetasa signifies both "reed" and "*phallus*."[25] This correspondence between phallus and reed (or *stambha*) suggests affinity with Śiva, who is sometimes portrayed as a column or pillar. It is Śiva in his stambha form that *Bhagīratha* worships for the gift of Gaṅgā. Furthermore, Śiva is characterized as Lord of the *Liṅgam*, a word popularly translated as phallus. Although Vedic orthodoxy dondemns those who worship the phallus, the very force of their imprecations suggests its popularity. In one passage, Indra is urged to keep them far from the sacrifice. In another he slays them after storming their castle.[26]

But whether as lingam or pillar, worship of the stone column undergoes the same tendencies as other numinous objects, absorbing the values of the *indigenous* people. The *Ṛg-Veda* addresses itself "to him even in the rock and in the house: Immortal One, he cares for all mankind." Line the tree, the pillar develops from a burial marker into a dwelling place of god, charged with the powers of life. Similarly, as the *tomb* of earth is a mother, so its circle of stones becomes a womb, protitious to birth and its renewal.[27] Accordingly a bracelet - shaped like the female organ - is invoked for its power of fertility.[28] At the same time, the pillar is equated with the organ of generation. Prajāpati the creator, desiring increase, "stretched out for himself that stone which projects. With that he impregnated [woman]. Her lap is a sacrificial alter.[29] Due perhaps to its generative association,

---

25 Madanjeet Singh, *Himālayan Art* (New York, 1968), p. 102.

26 Such as *Tiruvannamallai*, See G. Jouveau - Duabreuil, Iconography of Southern India (Paris, 1937), p. 12.

27 See *Mireca Eliade*, Patterns in Comparative Religion (Cleveland, 1963), pp. 231-232.

28 *Frankfort*, Births of Civilization in the Near East, p. 56.

29 *Stella Kramrisch*, The Hindu Temple (Calcutta, 1946), vol. 1, p. 161.

the pillar evolves from burial marker to *stambha* to *liṅgam*, the main object of worship in the *Hindu temple.*

The relation between the lingam and Śiva - or what archaeologists call the *Proto - Śiva* - extends to the *Indus Valley civilization*, where several remains, such as the round stone caps at *Harappa* and the well-known seal of the *polycephalic yogī*, have let scholars to attribute a primordial native origin to the Lord of the Liṅgaṁ. Despite Vedic condemnation, the liṅgaṁ as *stambha* retains its generative quality, which in the *Mahābhārata* becomes Śiva's mark, acknowledged by all the gods.

Aside from his association with the liṅgām, Śiva fills several other roles as the temple atchetype. One is his strong connection with the burial ground, which first gave rise to the temple idea itself. In the epic, *Śiva* declares: 'I do not see any spot that is more sacred than the crematorium . . . of all abodes, the crematorium pleases my heard most.[30] *Yama*, god of death, receives his srewardship from *Śiva*.[31] At times *Śiva* temples were built upon the graves themselves. This custom may well explain why the architectural treatises specify their construction outside the village precincts.[32] A ninth-century inscription of the Çola king *Rājāditya* records the construction of a *Śiva* temple, built on the spot where the king's father was buried. The practice exists today in the south, but only for the more affluent; the less fortunate stillest up modest liṅgaṁs on the site.[33] Mrs. *Sindlair Stevenson* mentions a small *Śiva* temple in *Kathiawar* built on the spot where a local rājā had been burned and his bones buried. The shrine contained a *liṅgaṁ*, an image of *Śiva's* wife *Pārvatī*, and a statue of *Gaṅgā*.[34]

---

30 *Rāmāyana* V. 15.43.

31 Fleet, Corpus Inscriptionem Indicarum, vol. 3, p. 78; *Samarāngana* 55-3.

32 C.D. Diehl, Instrument and Purpose (Lund, Sweden, 1956), p. 254.

33 *E.B. Havell*, The *Himālayas* in Indian Art (London, 1924), p. 26.

34 *Walter Leifer*, Himalaya: Mountain of Destiny (London, 1962), p. 2.

Śiva and Mountain

Śiva, as a god of death and emblem of fertility, is also associated with the cosmic mountain. This identity is seen in his epithets, such as "he who dwells in the mountains." He is known variously as lord, protector, or friend of the mountain. The relationship is expressed in the names of his wife - *Pārvatī* and *Umā Haimavatī* both signifying the daughter of the mountain; it is visually portrayed by the image of *Gaṅgā* that accompanies him and who is also called Haimavati. In a world of endless permutation and equivalence, *lingam* and mountain coalesce. In the *Himālayas*, the *lingam* is called Dhruva, fixed or unmoving, a term describing the primordial unmovable *lingam* and the great mountains themselves.[35] In South India, whole mountains are regarded as lingams.[36] The conjoint theme of lingam and mountain corresponds to the Greek omphalos, which may incorporate the three functions of grave marker, fertility, and sacred mountain.[37] Thus, like Gaṅgā, Śiva becomes a god of the triple world, his symbol the trident often carried by his devotees.

The notion of mountain as a home of god, a common theme throughout the ancient world, culminates in the mountain built by human hands, the ziggurat (ca. 2000 B.C.). Its long flight of stairs was designed to receive the god, who descended from the summit. The names of different ziggurats - Home of the Mountain, Mountain of Storm, Bond between Heaven and Earth - leave no doubt of its prototype.[38] Moreover, it seems likely that ideas related to the mountain also served as a model for the Hindu temple. In the architectural manuals, *Meru* and *Kailua* appear as names for the most

---

35 *Lucien Levy* - Bruhl, How Natives Tbink (New York, 1966), p. 330.

36 Diehl, C.D. Instrument and Purpose, Lund Iweden 1956 p. 66.

37 *Agni Purāṇa* 102.17.

38 "Alter, 'pillar,' mountain, cave, enclosure and gate," says *Kramrisch* "Singly and conjointly they are the themes of sacred architecture in India, as they have been in the Mediterranean and Near Eastern civilizations since the days of *Megalithic* art." See The Hindu Temple, vol. 1, p. 16.

prominent types of temples.[39] Both literary evidence and inscriptions compare the temple to a mountain. In his search for *Rāma's* wife *Sītā*, Hanuman the monkey king comes upon "a splendid temple white as Mount Kailua . . . supported by a thousand pillars . . . and of such height that it seemed to kiss the sky." And again: "The temple was as high as the peak of *Meru*, and . . . resembled a mountain."[40] In a fifty-century inscription, a king's minister directs his sons to build a temple to Vishnu resembling the peaks of *Kailua*. Elsewhere Mount *Meru* itself is described as the king of temples. The temple ritual of circumambulation is sometimes performed about a sacred hill or mountain. Madras State, for example, has several hills ringed with prescribed paths for the pilgrim. They serve on a larger scale the same ritual purose as the temple.

Some people claim to find a linear resemblance between the magic mountains and the temple - for example, if "the side elevation of the *Kailua* Temple at *Ellora* is compared with the actual skyline of Kailua . . . it will be onvious that the temple desigtner was not relying upon his imagination only. He himself must have performed the greatest of all pilgrimages and his intention was to reproduce the exact build-up of the holy mountain. While such thoughts hover in the realm of speculation, the mountains have undoubtedly exerted their influence on the Indian mind since Vedic times, when they were already the home of the gods and the source of soma.

With the *Aryan* movement southeast into the *Gaṇges* Valley, the mountains are left behind; but their significance remains. Such conditions are favourable to both literary and architectural mythology, and there may be certain truth to one writer's statement that "*Kailua* temples were built everywhere in order to carry the

---

39 "The temple and statutes," says Kramrisch, "are so many stages in the approach to *moksha*. "See The Art of India (London, 1954), p. 10.

40 Similarly, in an architectural commentary the *Agni Purāṇa* (104. 29-30) indicares the evoloution from tree to pillar support at the entranceway: "The ornamental branches overhanging the doors should be made to culminate in the images of celestials."

Himālayas into the smallest villages. However, since the *Ṛg-Veda* reflects *Aryan* experience west of the *Indus* and nearere the *Hindu Kush, Kailua* may later have come to represent more" a *Himālaya* of the mind" than an architectonic model. The temple as symbolic mountain reflects Levy - Bruhl's contention that myth remains poorly developed when the cohesion of a social group is strong, for then participation in the group is actually lived. Myth arises when the group "endeavors to realize a participation no longer directly felt." To the extent that *Levy - Bruhl* is correct, the temple represents a fusion of *Vedic* and non-Vedic sources, since the Vedic mountain and the abode of Śiva are two diverse perceptions. Ultimkately *Mahādev* (*Śiva*) predominates, as the temple ritual is chiefly non-Aryan.

At the core of these ideas is *Śiva*. His association with the funeral ground, thelingam as an emblem of death and symbol of life, his identity with the mountain, his connection with the waters - all provide a blueprint for the symbolic and ritual design of the *Hindu* temple. According to the *Purāṇas*, the *temple* "should be contemplated as filled throughout with the essence of Śiva. In terms of symbolic architecture, the primary units of the temple include the building, the alter, the door, and the guardians. As we have seen, the building may be conceived as a mountain. Though various sects have different summits - *Kailua* for *Śaivites*, *Vaikunṭa* for *Vaiṣṇavas* - *Śiva's* mountain serfves most often for comparison. The sanctum of everyr *Śiva* temple, and many others as well, contains a lingam and yoni, stylized representations of *phallus* and *vulva*, which evolve from the slab and ring stones placed above the funeral mound. In literature the lingam is sometimes pictured as rising from a lake, an image that reflects the place of water in the structure and rites of the temple. In addition to the *yoni*, the water element is emphasized by the door guardians - especially *Gaṅgā* and *Yamunā* - and the role that *Gaṅgā* water plays in the temple ritual itself.

The indwelling deity of trees and pillars made them objects of worship in the *Mediterranean* world. With the evolution of structural architecture, first one and then the other came to be used as a building support throughout the temple and at the entranceway. With the development of iconic images, the door pillars - with their *anthropomorphic* quality - were transformed into guardians. The change occurred slowly; at *Eridu* in *Mesopotamia*, for example, sixteen levels of settlement (from about the fifth millennium B.C. to the rise of the ziggurat around 2000 B.C.) disclosed no human sculpture.[41]

The first guardians, like the genii and fabulous animals standing at the gates of *Assyrian* palaces, were terrifying figures. Even the cherubim at the Garden of *Eden* may have been minatory and foreboding.[42] Aside from the mystery religions, the *Mediterranean* world viewed the doorway as an entrance unto darkness. To the ancients, the Pillars or *Hercules* signified the farthest limits of the known world. Samson's pulling down the temple pillars (Judges 16:30) rcaffirms the Old Testament vision of redemption through death. Some of the Indian door guardians present the same fierce aspect.[43]

Just as India possessed a "*spirigualized architecture*," so it displayed a "spiritualized physiology." The *Hatbapradipika*, a yogic text from the fourteenth to eighteenth centuries, explains the portal of ascension: "The goddess *Gaṅgā* is *Iḍā* [referring to the *Soma* qualities], the river *Yamunā* is *Pingala* [of the *Agni traits*]. Between them lies the *Kuṇḍalinī* [the untapped source of spiritual energy resting at the base of the spinal cord]". To attain the sanctum, "the poor young ascetic widow [*Kuṇḍalinī* resting between *Gaṅgā* and *Yamunā*] should be caught by force [by the *yogī*]. That would be

41 *S.Giedion*, The Eternal Present, vol. 2: The Beginnings of Architecture (New York, 1964), p. 97.

42 See *Goblet d'Alviella*, The Migration of Symbols (New York, 1956), p. 153

43 Such as the *Ghatesvar temple*, Badoli. See Odette Viennot, Les Divinites fluriales *Gaṅgā* et Yamunā (Paris, 1964), p. 40a.

the highest stage.[44] Among the many yogic exercises recommended, this "brings about the confluence of the three currents [flowing in the three channels: *Iḍā*, *Pingalā*, and the center channel, the Susbumna] and carries the mind to *Kedāra* [*Kedārnāth*, the *Himālayan* shrine marking the confluence of the *Alkanandā* and the *Mandākini*, two of the three original tributaries of *Gaṅgā*][45] Here, in altered form, reappears the image of the *sangam* at *Prayag*, the point of mysticalk consciousness where the three rivers meet.

So important was the entranceway in South India that by the twelfth century monumental gateways (gopuras) became the largest and architecturally most significant structure of the temple.[46] In South Indian ritual, the priest may begin a ceremony by aksing permission of the Guardian of the Field (often himself a manifestation of *Śiva*) to enter the temple and worship *Mahādev* (*Śiva*). He then sprinkles water over the door as well as upon the guardians on either side.[47] In worshipping *Śiva*, one should first adore *Gaṅgā, Yamunā*, and *Sarasvatī* among the other gods and celestials.[48] After worshipping the river goddesses, the priest addresses the door, whose ultimate meaning is known through *Vedānta*, who has the shape ofall the worlds and is omnipresent.[49] The ritual relation between temple and water - especially water from the holy rivers - existed elsewhere in the ancient world. A ceremony at Babylon resembles the one described here, down to the mention of the two rivers. The priest is directed to draw water from the *Tigris* and *Euphrates* in two separate cisterns and with these sprinkle both the temple and the sanctuary.[50] The ceremony resembles the pouting of *Gaṇges* water on the *lingam*, a

---

44 *Hathapradipika* III. 106. The spinal cord itself is called the *Sushumnā*, a term equated in the text (III.4) with Śiva's burning ground.

45 Ibid. III. 23

46 *J.C.Harle*,Temple Gateway in South India (Oxford, 1963). p. viii.

47 *Diehl*, Instruments and Purpose, p. 106.

48 *Agni,* P. 21. 9-11.

49 Diehl, p. 106.

50 James Pritchard (ed). Ancient Near Eastern Texts (Princeton, 1955), pp.331, 333.

rite in Indian tradition that duplicates the descent of the rivers from the holy mountain. We will now examine both these themes.

The Mountain and the Waters

In the *Ṛg-Veda*, the mountains are the home of water: of rivers, of rain, of soma - all forms of the life - conferring liquid (*amrita*). At that time the mountains were portrayed as holding back the water laden clouds which lay hidden among them. Gradually the theme recedes and the mountains - notably Himavat (*Himālaya*) - are characterized as the home of the rivers. The relation between *Gaṅgā* and *Himālaya*, mentioned throughout the epics and *Purāṇas*. Frequently in Indian literature *Gaṅgā* is spedifically connected with *Kailua*, *Śiva's* mountain, and with *Meru*, where he sometimes dwells.[51] Along with other rivers, *Gaṅgā, Sarasvatī, Sindhu* (*Indus*), and *Yamunā* are described as flowing from theslopes of Himavar.[52] In fact, several *Purāṇas* mention the entire river system of Asia as rising in theregion of Menu and flowing from there to the corners of theearth - after rirst separating from *Gaṅgā*.[53] Sometimes *Gaṅgā* falls directly on the head of *Śiva* before dividing into its several streams.[54] from this wealth of mythology emerges the further correspondence between *Śiva* and the mountain - conjointly the origin of the rivers, with *Gaṅgā* the formost.

Gaṅgā and the mountains were regarded as a source of life and sustenance. The Arthāśāstra (late fourth to early third centuries B.C.) recommends that in time of drought one should worship Indra, *Gaṅgā*, the mountains, and the sea.[55] *Gaṅgā's* relation to Śiva evolves naturally from *Gaṅgā* and *Himālaya*, especially with the emergence of the *Śiva-liṅgaṁ* as the embodiment of the magic mountain.

---

51 Mhh. III. 144; also the Tibetan Kailua Purana. See Swami Pranavananda, Kailua-Mansarovar (Calcutta, 1949), p. 8 See also Markandeya P. 56. 7-9; Kurma, p. 1`.44.7.

52 *Mārkaṇḍeya,* p. 57. 18.

53 *Viṣṇu,* P. II.2 and II.8; *Bhāgavata* P. 5.17; *Kūrma,* p. 1.44.28-33.

54 *Viṣṇu,* P. II. 1 and II.8; *Bhāgavata* P. 5.17; *Kūrma,* p. 1.44.28-33.

55 Ibid

Thus the ritual of pouring water on the *lingam* duplicates the river's descent from Himavat and the semen (*amṛita*) flowing from *Mahādev's* endless powers of generation. Seen in thiks light, Śiva's two consorts - *Gaṅgā and Umā - Pārvatī* - become declensikons of the archetypal *Himālayan* river, since *Umā* and *Pārvatī*, along with *Gaṅgā*, are often described as daughters of Himavat.[56] In his poem The Cloud Messednger, *Kālidāsa* fuses the image of *Śiva* and the mountain. The poet points the direction of the cloud across the high peaks (*Gauri* is another name for *Pārvatī*) :

Fly then where Gaṅgā on the king of mountains
Falls like a flight of stairs from heaven let down
For the sons of men; she hurls her billowy fountains
Like hands to grasp the moon on Śiva's crown
And laughs here foamy laugh at Gauri's jealous frown.
The Cloud Messenger 50

The relation between the mountains and the waters is further reflected in the image of the lotus. "The *lotus* is the waters," says the *Brahmāha*.[57] From it rises *Meru*, the primeval mountain. This theme underlies the custom of surrounding the temple with an artificial body of water (as at Mārtand and the Golden Temple at Amritsar) The lotus as the womb duplicates the *yoni*, the foundation of the lingam.[58] Thus the sanctum is founded on the waters. Its name *garbba-grihya* (House of the Womb) is embodied in the yoni and ritualized by the pouring of *Gaṅgā* water.

56 *Ranataba* 1,351 Jeba Yo, III.25.

57 SB vii. 4.1.8.

58 SB X. 5.2.7-89. "The entrance of the *garbha-gṛihya*," says *Kramrisch*, "is the sculptural metamorphosis of the natural tirtha." See The Hindu Temple, vol. 2, p. 315. In *Egypt*, "In naissance ou la renaissance par le *lotus* . . . est un theme de i'iconographic et de la liturgie de tous les dieux." See A. Moret, "Le lotus et la naissance des dieux," Journal Asiatique 9 (1917): 505.

The Liṅgam and the Waters

The delightful *Kathasaritsāgara* (Ocean of Story) from the tenth or eleventh century relates the tale of a woman who stood beside a lake, praying to *Mahādev*. "And *Śiva* rose from the lake . . . in the form of a *linga*.[59] In the *Rāmāyaṇa*, the demon *Rāvaṇa* emereges from a bath in the *Narmadā* River and leads a ceremonial procession. "Wherever the Lord of the *Rākshasas* went, a golden *Śiva-linga* was borne before him.[60] The relationship between the *lingam* (mountain, pillar) and the waters already appears in the *Brāhmaṇas*, where the stones encircling the burial mound are equated with the water. The sacrificer "thus surrounds this world with water.[61] We glimpse it again in the *Upaniṣads*, whee "he who was born of old from *tapas* [austerities] was born from water.[62] Although the *Upaniṣad* is referring here to *Atman*, it is *Śiva* who later becomes the ideal *tapaspati*, Master of *Austerities*.[63] The *lingam* and its effluents are coextensive. "Who is it whose semen was offered in the sacrifice in the beginning of the world? . . . Is the golden mountain [*Meru*] made of any other *seman*? . . . See how the world bears everywhere the signature of the *liṅgaṁ* and the yoni.[64] We come upon the story of *Rāma*, his brother *Lakshmaṇa, Sītā*, and the monkey king *Hanumān*, crossing Rameshvara Island (near Sri Lanka) after defeating the demon *Ravaṇa*. There they stopped to worship and adorn the well-known *Rāma Lingam* "that Hanuman

---

59 *Kathāsaritsāgara* XVIII. 70.171.

60 VII. 31.

61 SB VII. 1.1.12

62 Bhāgavata P. IV. 24.14

63 Bhāgavata P. IV. 24.14.

64 Mbh. XIII, 14. According to Cope, "the traditional Christian font-rituals . . . give full expression to the sexual aspect of the regenerative process of baptism. The font is unmistakably a *womb*, and in the Holy Saturday ceremonies the Paschal candle signifies the contribution of the masculine spirit. The massive candle is plunged three times into the font, and in some rites, the liquid wax is made to drip into the water. "See Gilbert Cope, Sym-bolism in the Bible and ibe Church (New York, 1959), p. 102.

had brought from the *Gaṇges*."[65] The story may represent a local legend, since it is not attested by any *Rāma lingams* on early South Indian temples. If so, it further emphasizes the association of *Śiva* with the river goddess, at thie pont far distant from the source. At all events, the connection between *Gaṅgā* and the *lingam* has become inseparable, as indicated by themodern guidebook issued to pilgrims at the *Rameshvaram* temple.

One of the public rituals in the South Indian temple involves a ceremonial bath in which *Śiva* is taken to a sleeping chamber outside the sanctum. During the procession, *Gaṅgā*, who lives in the god's matted hair, flees at the sight of *Śiva's* wife *Pārvatī*. From that hour, all sacred water places or *tirthas* become *Gaṅgā's* abode and for that reason are considered holy. "In order to bring here back to *Śiva's* hair, she is made to enter a vessel filled with river water. The vessel is then decorated . . . and carried on the head of an elephant or ... a temple servant" to the accompaniment of music.[66] It is brought to the *lingam* and poured over it. The watere falling on the lingam is collected in the *yoni*, then carried from the shrine though a small channel that sometimes ends in a *Makara* or cow's head.[67] Inside, the wall above the water drain may contain a figure of *Gaṅgā*, which is worshipped during temple ceremonies.

Still another theme connects the waters and the temple. A long Bengali poem about the goddess *Chanḍī* describes the building of a temple. "In the course of a single night, the temple was constructed by *Vishvakarman* [the celestial architect] . . . The waters of the river *Bhagavatī* [*Gaṅgā* in the netherworld] oozed up to fill the tanks." The samed event is mentioned by the poet *Bharatachandra* of the *Pātāla-Gaṅgā*, filling the tank or pool of a newly created temple.[68]

---

65 Jouveau-Dubreuil, Iconography of Southern India, p. 16.

66 Diehl, op. cit. p. 241.

67 Stevenson, Rites of the Twice-Born, p. 375.

68 Tamonash Das Gupta, Aspects of Bengali Society from Old Bengali Literature (Calcutta, 1935), pp. 111-112. A story in the *Kathāsaritsāgara* (IX.56) describes the adventures of *Nala*, famous for his skill in chariot driving and

The tradition is difficult to interpret. It may express the same relationship as the burial marker and the *womb* of the waters, the reciprocity of death and life. It also bears some resemblance to the *Vedic hymns* in which the cleft mountain releases the waters. In this respect, it may represent a ritual designed to ensure the flow of the river for agricultural purposes.

The Merging of Dualities

With the rise of the *Gupta dynasty* in the fifth century, the age of temple building begins. As we have seen, the Hindu temple evolves from several different antecedents reaching back to the origins of *Indian civilization.* The sapling, the tumulus, the stone slab, and the pillar-announcing the place of the dead-come to house the departed spirit and eventually the deathless god himself, embodied in the lingam. This mark of potency stands at the center of the temple, the center of the world mountain. Surrounding the central point is the ring of stones - the shape of mother earth, the *lotus*, the waters - evolved into the yoni that ultimately gives birth to the creator. The parts of the temple are conceived in apposition and embellishment this single theme - the merging of dualities: male and female, fire and water, left and right, *Gaṅgā* and *Śiva*. As the contrast to *Mahādev*, the river goddess appears as a door guardian; *Gaṇges* water poured on the *lingam* often flows from the temple through an opening shaped like a *Makara* (*Gaṅgā's vehicle*) or a cow (the river begins at *Gomukh*, meaning the mouth of the cow). Above the drain may be found an image of *Gaṅgā* herself.

---

cooking The hero is bitten by a snake and his body is inhabited by a black figure named *Kāli*, tantamount to dying. Eventually he recovers from the snakebite, frees himself from the demon, and finds employment as a cook. His skillis such that "waters gushed up in pots and pans without being put in." Here Nala's recovery may be seen as a return from the dead, the waṭers as those of the underworld.

In art, the goodess is portrayed in free standing statuary and in several other forms. But her best-known representation is at the entrance to the temple, where her life-conferring image is enhanced by the sculptured omaments that normally are accompany and surround *Gaṅgā* the divine origin.

CHAPTER 2

GAṄGĀ, THE MYTH AND HER ORIGIN

Stories from Indian mythology seem to have endured in rural culture for millennia, buttressed by a myriad of annotations. The noted Indian novelist *R.K. Narayan*, a fine storyteller, saw the legends of the eighteenth major *Purāṇas* retold by the village raconteur as emblematic of the extended moral universe of the *Vedas* and the *Upaniṣads*. For Narayan's storyteller, "stories, scriptures, ethics, philosophy, grammar, astrology, astronomy, semantics, mysticism and moral codes" were interrelated as part of a larger whole - keys to understanding life and existence.[69] This great tradition was alive in the humblest corners of village India, where rural folk who did not have access to classical Sanskrit or the finer esoteric points of scripture could still partake of the lasting moral vision of a higher social order.

The stories, of course, are never quite the same. Not only is each telling slightly different, but many renditions run against the grain of the original epics and their intended moral lessons. In other words, a living mythical past is not sustained by mere

69 Narayan, R. K., God, Demons and others, Chicago, 1993, p.4.

replication: far more capricious forces are at work. Poet, scholar, and translator extraordinaire A.K. Ramanujan, commenting on the multiple versions of the *Rāmāyaṇa* that coexist across the cultures and languages of the Indian subcontinent, saw the prevalence of a particular set of texts in a given culture as a common "pool of signifiers."[70] This was true of oral traditions that sustained a perennial epic imagination with a repository of plots, characters, names, geographies, incident, relationships, phrases, proverbs, and insults. Indian remains a culture steeped in stories and story telling, in which folk and classical traditions have been entwined for a long time. Indian epics like the *Mahābhārata* have thus absorbed over millennia and encyclopedic range of folk minutiae - tales, beliefs, and proverbs. As Ramanujan also pointed out, the oral and folk traditions in turn continually redact, refurbish, and redistribute this material across different regional, local, and linguistic registers.[71] In this regard, much like the ancient Greek myths described my Marcel Detienne, the Indian traditions must have been more exegetical than interpretative. Their interlocutors have been engaged over since in a continuous and lively disquisition, spinning disarming critiques of their own moral standards, symbols, behaviors, and practices.[72]

Perhaps the most frequented source of the story of the descent of the *Gaṅgā* is found in India's popular and venerable epic, the *Rāmāyaṇa*. Sage *Vālmiki*, to whom the oldest surviving version of the epic is attributed, was moved to utter the first lines of his verse near the confluence of the *Gaṅgā* and its tributary, the *Tamasa*, when he was distressed by the sight of a huntsman taking aim at two cranes (*krauṅcamithuna*) flying together over the sandbanks and bringing down one of the pair, and was moved deeply by its mate's piteous

70 Ramanujam, A.K., Three Hundred Rāmāyaṇ, five plus and three though on Translated (ed) many Rāmāyaṇa Berkeley 1991, p. 46.

71 Detienne, Marcel the Greeks and us of comparative , 2007, p.29.

72 *Detienne*, Marcel the Greeks and us comparative Anthropology of Ancient Grace, Coambridge, 2007, p.29.

cries.[73] The site of the composition of the *Rāmāyaṇa* is thus not far from the shores of the *Gaṅgā* and its floodplains. Today, a section of the River *Tāmasa*, known colloquially as the *Toṇs*, runs through the present-day Mau district of Uttar Pradesh, along the fertile plains of the tract between the *Gaṅgā* and its tributary, the *Ghāghyarā* (also known as the *Gaṅgā - Ghāgharā Doab*), about sixty miles east of Varanasi. The domicile of Rāma's father. King *Daśaratha*, in *Ayodhya* was a city on the banks of the *Sarayū*, which was most likely the name for a section of the River Ghāghara back then. During his exile, *Rāma*, *Lakṣmaṇa*, and *Sītā* visited the meeting point of the *Gaṅgā* and the *Yamunā* at *Prayāg* and crossed the *Gaṅgā* into the forests of its southern banks. In other words, the *Gaṅgā* appears in many guises in the epic. It is not just a mythical river that fell from the heavens. It is also part of the natural setting for the story that lends a geographical familiarity and spatial orientation to its larger plot. In *Vālmiki's Rāmāyaṇa*, the story of the *Gaṅgā* is told by the great sage *Viṣvāmitra* to *Rāma* and *Lakṣmana*.

Rāma and his brother were sent as young boys to *Viṣvamitra's* for est sanctuary (Āśrama) to protect the forest-dwelling ascetics from demons who kept disrupting their sacrificial rituals. Toward the end of their stay, the sage decided to accompany them to the principality of *Mithilā*, where a sumptuous sacrifice had been arranged by King *Janaka*. On the way they crossed the River Shona, and in a day's journey they came to the *Gaṅgā*. The brothers were delighted to see the holy waters of the *Gaṅgā* (*puṇyasalilam*) and here banks where wild geese and white cranes flocked.[74] After they had bathed in the river and offered their prayers to ancestors. *Rāma* asked the great sage about the origins of the *Gaṅgā*. "How does she traverse the three worlds to come at last to the ocean, lord of rivers and streams?"[75]

---

73 Vālmīki's Rāmāyaṇ book one, Beyond, Trans. Robert P. Goldaman, New York 2005, pp. 45-47.

74 Sen, Sudiplo Gaṅgā, the ways past of river, Gurgaon, 2019, pp. 52-54.

75 Ibid.

The sage then narrated the story of the river to these two young princes from *Ayodhya. Himālaya*, lord of the great mountain ranges of the north, had two beautiful daughters. Their mother was the daughter of Mount *Meru*, the axis of earth. *Gaṅgā* was the elder, and the younger one was Umā. During the struggle between the gods and demons, Śiva, the great warrior and leader of the divine army, had taken up the life of an ascetic while his wife, Umā, had taken up a stint of severe penance. The gods were afraid of rushing into battle without Śiva. In their desperation to end the meance of demons, the gods banded together and appealed to *Gaṅgā* - the river that passes through heaven, earth, and the netherworld - for help. They asked her for an offspring that would be supremely pure and brave worthy of the looming great battle with the demons. *Gaṅgā's* father, *Himālaya*, consented to give her away for this purpose. And that is how, *Viṣvāmitra* explained, *Gaṅgā* came down from heaven to earth. *Rāma* listened attentively to this explanation but was still not satisfied. He wanted to know more about Gaṅgā. Where did she come from? Why does she flow in three separate dimensions ?

The sage went on. *Śiva*, the "dark-throated one,"[76] once desired the goddess *Gaṅgā* and lay with her for a hundred celestial years, but their union bore no fruit. The gods were concerned about a child of *Śiva*, the god of destruction, because of his fearsome potency. *Śiva* assured them that he would refrain from begetting a child, but he could not stop the spilling of his semen. The gods asked the earth to receive his seed, and from this mountains and forests came into being. The god of fire, *Agni*, helped transform *Śiva's* sperm into a lustrous white mountain, from which a son, *Kārttikeya* would be born. However, *Śiva's* wife, *Umā*, could not bear this, and she put a curse on the gods so that none of them would be able to have children ever again. Alarmed by this, the gods beseeched *Brahmā*, the forebear of all gods. Brahmā told them that *Umā's* curse could not be undone, and indeed they would not be able to father children; however, *Agni*, the fire god, should beget a child with Uma's curse

76 *Śiva* referred to as *Nilankantsha* (Blue throats)

couldnot be undone, and indeed they would not be able to father children: however, *Agni*, the fire god, should beget a child with Uma's sister, *Gaṅgā*, the river-goddess, who would grow up to be a great solider and flght for the gods against demons.

Gaṅgā agreed to this as well, and Agni, captivated by here enchanting beauty, proceeded to consummate the union. Alas, the embryo was too fiery for her to bear. *Agni* asked *Gaṅgā* to place it at the foot of the Himālayas. The embryo had the "luster of molten gold," and as it came in contqact with the earth it was transformed into various elements. The mountains and the forest were turned to gold. The child was nurtured by the gods, who sent maidens from heaven (*Kṛittikās*) to nurse him. The boy was named both *Kārttikeya* (because he had been mothered by the *Kṛittikās*) and Skanda, and just as *Brahmā* had foretold, he became a mighty warrior who single handedly demolished entire clans of demons.

Different versions of the story of the conception of *Kārttikeya* appear later in the *Mahābhārata* and the *Brahmavaivarta Purāṇa*, but the *Gaṅgā* does not feature as prominently in these renditions.[77] The telling of this story in *Vālmīki's Rāmāyaṇ* is thus of great interest to its. Not only does *Gaṅgā* appear here as the sister of Śiva's consort and daughter of the *Himālayas*, but there is a subtle interweaving of whims and desires of the gods and the alignment of natural forces. The mountains, forests water, and elements appear in the guise of deities. The *Himālayas* are real mountains, but they are also the resting place of *Śiva*, the reclusive, scandalous ascetic and his fearsome and ghoulish companions. The *Gaṅgā* is a river like any other. Its banks are skirted with lush forests that shelter birds and animals of every description and provide refuge to ascetics and holy men. Yet the same *Gaṅgā* is also a daughter of the mountains, an enticing beauty who violates *Śiva's* meditation and arouses his lust. She is the mother of *Kārttikeya*. She is pure and unsullied, and only she can bear a child sired by *Agni*, the god of fire.

---

77 *Vālmīki's Rāmāyaṇa*, Book I, p. 211.

There was much more to the story that *Viṣvāmitra* had started to narrate. As we shall see, *Gaṅgā* was eventually persuaded to water the plains below the *Himālayas* - not because of divine caprice after all, but through the acts of a worthy and virtuous man. This man would have to suffer impossible ordeals, yet remain unṣaken in his resolve to purge the sins of his ancestors. This was *Bhagīratha*, who belonged to the royal line of *Ayodhya*, as did Rama. And because *Bhagīratha* succeeded in coaxing the celestial river to flow through human habitations and bless the earth with her endless bounty, the *Gaṅgā* also came to be known as *Bhāgirathī*. In its eastern stretch, the *Gaṅgā* is still called by that name.

Gaṅgā to the Earth

A righteous and brave king of *Ayodhyā* called King *Sāgara* had two beautiful wives, *Keshinī* (the one with lustrous hair) and *Sumati* (the well intentioned). *Sagara* was childless. Driven by the quest for a child, he and his wives visited the Himalayas to perform austerities lot a hundred human years. Pleased by such dedication, the great sage *Bhṛigu* granted the king a boon. He and his wives would be blessed with children, and he would attain unrivaled fame in the world. One wife would bear sixty thousand sons, and the other would give birth to the one who would carry on the dynasty. The sage left it up to the two wives. *Keshinī* wanted her son to be the scion who would keep the lineage, and *Sumati* chose to be the mother of a multitude of sons. Keshini gave birth to a son, *Asamanja*, *Sumati* delivered a fetal mass from which sixty thousand male infants emerged. This great band of brother grew up to be strong and handsome men. *Keshinī's* son *Asamanja*, as he became older, turned into a rogue and a meance to the inhabitants of *Ayodhya*, seizing children and drawing them in the waters of the *Sarayu* for sport. His father had to eventually banish him from the city. *Asamanja* had a son named *Aṁsumant* (*Angshuman*), who became known for his kindness and breavery.

Now *Sagara*, the aging king, decided to perform the great sacrificial rite of *Aśvamedha*, in which a royal white stallion was let loose, followed by the king's troops. Wherever the horse ran unchallenged, the king would claim his dominion. King *Sāgara's* horse was guarded by Prince *Aṁshumant* astride a great chariot with his bow at the ready. However, *Indra*, the lord of all the gods, decided to play a trick on Aṁshumant and his retinue and teach them a lesson. He took the shape of ademon and carried off the sacrificial horse. This was distressing news for the king. A defective horse-sacrifice would surely incur the wrath of the gods and bring disaster on the king and his progeny. *Sāgara* beseeched his sons to pursue and seize the horse by any means possible. "You must dig up the very earth itself until the horse is found," he said.[78]

As the command, *Sāgara's* sons began to tear up the corners of the earth with great fury, molesting and scattering a multitude of netherworld dwellers: gods, *demons, ogres*, and *serpents*. In sheer terror they fled to Brahma, praying that he might stop this wanton destruction of the innocent denizens of the underworld (*rasātala*). *Brahmā* assured them that this misfortune had been preordained, and that *Sagara's* sons would soon pay a terrible price for their misdeeds. Meanwhile, though they had dug up the earth in every direction and destroyed countless creatures, *Sagara's* sons had not yet found the horse thief. In another version of this story that appears in the Bhagavata Purana, the ocedans of the world were created by the earth being dug up by *Sagara's* sons during their frenzied search.[79]

Indra, king of the gods, had actually run away with the sacrificial horse and taken it to the subterranean Ashram of the famous sage and philosopher Kapila, where it grazed. Eventually *Sāgara's* sixty thousand sons arrived at this sanctuary and spotted their missing stallion. Thinking that *Kapila* had stolen the horse and blinded by fury, they tried to attach him. *Kapila*, livid at this affront, glared at the intruders and, uttering the word "hut," incinerated them instantly

---

78 *Vālmīki's Rāmāyaṇa*, Book I, p. 219.

79 Sinha Purnendy Nārāyaṇa Sinha, A Study of the *Bhāgarvata Purāṇa* in Estoric Hinduism, Varanasi 1901, p.196.

into a heap of ashes.[80] The only one left now to look for the horse was the king's grandson, *Aṁshumant*, Following the trail of destruction left by *Sāgara's* sons, he quickly reached the netherworld and found the remains of his kinsmen. Overcome by grief, he looked around for water to perform libations for the last rites, but he found no source of water nearby. At this time *Suparṇā*, the king of birds who lived in the nearby forest, stepped forward to console *Amshumant*. He told him not to grieve and to accept the late that had befallen his clan. He also told him that no earthly water could be offered as libation for deliverance of these poor souls. Their ashes must be washed with the waters of *Gaṅgā*, the eldest daughter of *Himālaya*, and only then would the spirits of his slain kinsfolk be set free.

Thus a terrible burden now rested on the progeny of *Sāgara*. How to bring down the *Gaṅgā* from the faraway heavens to the netherworld? Neither *Sagara* nor his grandson, *Aṁshumant*, could fathom this in their lifetime. *Aṁshumant's* son *Dilīpa* took up the cause and attempted to appease the divine forces with a severe regime of austerities on one of the mountain peaks of the *Himālayas*, which is said to have lasted for 3,200 years. Despite such resolve and penance, *Dilīpa* was not able to receive the right favor from the gods, nor did he succeed in coming up with a remedy for the funerary rites and salvation of his ancestors. All though his life he was preoccupied with one thought: "How can I bring down the Ganges? How can I perform these funeral libations [*jalakriyā*]? After his death, his son *Bhagīratha* became the king, and this became the mission of his life as well.

Bhagīrathā could not beget any sons. To win the favor of the gods he went to the *Gokarṇa* Mountain as a humble ascetic and began a long period of austerity. He kept his arms raised at all times, are only once, and succeeded in extinguishing all sensual desires. Much pleased with such virtuous behavior, *Brahmā*, the creator of the universe, granted him a special favor. He ordained that the wates of the *Gaṅgā* would come down from the heavens and wash

80 Sen Sudipta op cit; p. 54 and also *Vālmīki Rāmāyaṇa*, Book I, pp. 230-31.

the ashes of *Bhagīratha's* ancestors, releasing their spirits for their final resting place. The only condition was that the great Shiva must check the fall of mighty Gaṅgā, daughter of the mountains, once she plunged to this earth. Hearing this, *Bhagīratha*, in order to pay homage to the idiosyncratic *Śiva*, stood on the tip of one big toe for a whole year. Pleased at his painful supplication, *Śiva* agreed to bear the mighty *Gaṅgā* on his head. And thus Haimavati, the "snow-clad" daughter of the mountains, assumed the natural form of the river Gaṅgā, fel from the skies with thundering force onto *Śiva's* head, and rushed into the various coils of his copious and matted locks. This was mighty labyrinth from which she could not escape, and she splashed about in his curls for a number of years. *Śiva* was pleased by this an eventually released the river into a pool called *Bindu*, from where her waters rushed down to earth in fearsome roar. A host of gods and beavenly creatures came to watch this marvel and pay their obeisance. The *Rāmāyaṇa* provides a vivid account of the cascade of waters on earth in this passage:

> *The cloudless sky was shining with the hosts of hastening gods and the splendor of their ornaments, so that it was illumined by a hundred suns. Filled with masses of twisting snakes, crocodiles and fish, the sky seemed shot with scattered lightning. Now white with a thousand shreds of flying foam and flocks of snowy geese, the sky seemed suddenly filled with autumn clouds. At somepoints the river flowed swiftly, at others slowly, in some places it moved tortuously or broadened out; at others, it narrowed and sank between its banks only to rise elsewhere. Here and tghere the water dashed back upon itself, momentarily hurled up into the air, only tol fall to earth once more.*[81]

Because they fell from Śiva's locks, the waters were absolutely pure (toyam nirmalam) and had the power to wash away all sins. All came to bathe in the Gaṅgā, including the accursed who had been banished from heaven, and rejoiced as the waters bore their

81 Valmiki's *Rāmāyaṇa*, p. 239.

sins away. At the head of the rushing waters, mighty *Bhagīratha* rode, mounted on a celestial chariot, followed by gods, seers, and demons. Finally, on theirway to the ocean, the waters of the *Gaṅgā* flooded the creater where *Bhagīratha's* ancestors had been turned to ashes. *Brahmā* then apoke cirectly to *Bhagīrathā*, assuring him that *Sāgara's* sons would now ascend to heaven as gods, and the *Gaṅgā* would be known as his own daughter bearing his very name - *Bhāgirathī.*

Most of these narratives of Gaṅgā's plunge to the earth tghus intersperse their mythical accounts with a conscious invocation of natural imagery. The earliest interlocutors of this tale were well aware of the extensive riparian landscape associated with the Gaṅgā: glacial melts, watersheds, meanders, sandbanks, and the long journey of the river to its delta and the ocean.

VARIATIONS ON A THEME

How old is this story of the descent of the *Gaṅgā*? Historians have debated the dates of the compositions of the great epics *Rāmāyaṇa* and *Mahābhārata* at least since the advent of antiquarian scholarship during the early period of British rule in India. Today, scholars seem to agree that the compilation of the *Rāmāyaṇa* as a distant corpus can be traced back to a stretch of time between the fourth or fifth century B.C. and the third century B.C. Cities and kingdoms mentioned in the *Mahābhārata* located in the upper tracts of the *Gaṅgā - Yamunā* Doab, seem to have been settled earlier than the lower *Gaṅgā* plains where the *Rāmāyaṇa* unfolds. The *Mahābhārata* in its present outline probably took shape sometime between the fourth century B.C.E. and the fourth century BC Mythiks of the origins of the *Gaṅgā* can be found in bits and pieces in both these ep;ics and also in many of the eighteen major *Purāṇas*. Such stories, embedded in an extensive oral tradition and recounted in popular memory, clearly acquired a coherent or consistent form centuries before they were rendered into written tests.

The *Purāṇas* are said to have beenn put into writing by the first sages, beginning with *Vyāsa* during a time beyond human reckoning. They contain stories of the creation and re-creation of the universe; cycles of the primordial ancestor of humans, the *Manus*; the rise and fall of clans and dynasties; genealogies of gods and their deeds that shaped the world; lineages of ancient sages: and accounts of major dynasties.[82] The *Purāṇas* existed long before the advent of the Christian era and were written down as texts after the early first millennium C.E. Even afterward they continued as part of the recitative tradition of genealogy, guarded closely by Indian bards and rhapsodists (*sūtas*). At times they were written anew under the auspices of different rulers and tweaked for the pleasure of dynasties that patronized particular versions, especially in the interest of their own favored deities. A vast body of disparate narratives was absorbed into the corpus of the *Purāṇas* before the first compilations were put together. They were being restructured and recast as late as the Gupta period and after. The freedom with which the *Purāṇas* have been revised and rewritten creates serious limitations to their exact dating, leading to wild variations in the speculative date of individual texts, such as those of the *Bhāgavata Purāṇa*.[83]

Nevertheless, they make up the largest part of Sanskrit literature - a bewildering mass of text bustling with genealogy, cosmology, and history precipitated through centuries of collective recall. They are always in the process of revision, and the currently identifiable versions can be traced not much further beyond the fourth and fifth centuries B.C. Some scholars view them as corrupted forms of older standardized versions. Some evidence suggests that new versions have appeared as late as the eighteenth century. Given such variability and the virtuousity of both oral and written forms, it is not surprise that versions of the story of the descent of the *Gaṅgā* abound in the different *Purāṇas*, as they do in the *Rāmāyaṇa* and

82 The *Purāṇa's* are supposed to have five major identifying characters, *Sarga*, Prati sarga, *Vaṁsa*, *Manvantava* and *Vainsance charita*.

83 Pocher, *Purāṇas*, pp. 102, 147-148.

the *Mahābhārata*. No doubt these stories are connected. As one may well expect, there is an organic relationship between these specific episodes and the flow of the major epics. A comparison of versions shows how frequently the same segments of narrative appear. They are a testimony to both the resilience of the mythic form and the shared practices of the storytellers of Indian antiquity.

In the *Bhāgavata Purāṇa* attributed to the sage *Krișṇa - Dvaipāyana Vyāsa*, *Gaṅgā* appears in the form of a river adored by all three major deities *Brahmā*, *Viṣṇu* and Śiva. She is borne by *Brahmā* in the water pot for his ablutions. She is the consort of Śiva. She seeks sanctuary at *Viṣṇu's* feed, from where she eventually emerges, heeding the call of *Bhagīratha*, who needs her for the last rites of his ancestors.

> King *Bhagīratha* sounded his conch
> *Gaṅgā* rushed forward, but could not find a path
> and thus she lay there for a year
> Grief stricken, *Bhagīratha* blamed his fate.[84]

According to this Purāṇa, had been preordained in the saga of all creation that Gaṅgā will appear one day from above for the salvation of all humankind (*manavan sarvvan*) in theform of water on earth at the beseeching of the great *Bhagīrathā*.[85]

Lord *Krișṇa* says in the *Brahmavaivarta Purāṇa* that *Gaṅgā* water has the power to absolve the bad fruits of *karma* acquired by an individual over the course of many lifetimes.[86]

---

84 See Rudraraman Mitra's Bengali version of *Bhāgavata Purāṇa* and also *R. Mitra, Mahābhāgavata Purāṇa, Mahṛṣi Krishna Dvaipayana Pranita*, Calcutta 1893-1894, pp. 162-63.

85 Sanskrit original Udharattung Manavas Sarvan Jahnavi Parirupuni Jagama Tada bhumace *bhagīratha* Sevita in *Gaṅgā* appears on Earth because of the ministration of *Bhagīratha* by R. Mitra (ed) *Mahabhgāvata purāṇa*, Calcutta 1893-1894, pp. 162 - 163.

86 *Brahymavai Vartapuranam* (ed) by Panchanan Tarakaratha, Calcutta, 1917, p. 81.

It was always destined that *Bhagīrathā* would be the first to receive and worship *Gaṅgā* on earth. Humankind had been waiting thorough 5,000 dark years of the *Kaliyuga*. *Bhagīrathā* was the dutiful descendant of *Sagara*, who went through great physical pain and spiritual anguish to rescue the condemned souls of his ancestors by bringing *Gaṅgā* down to earth. In doing so, he gave humankind a way to wash away the debris of their sinful deeds. The *Bhagīratha Purāṇa* also explains why the *Gaṅgā* is a river so blessed. Not only does she splash around in *Śiva's* dreadlocks and in Brahma's ablution pot, she also hides for a while in *Viṣṇu's* eternal lotus feet. At one point Krishna, Vishnu's most recognizable avatar on earth, embraced the beautiful river on his felt flank, alienating his own-consort, *Rādhā*. The *Skanda Purāṇa* insists that the waters of the Gaṅgā are nothing but the essence of *Śiva's* potency, created and let loose for all falled creatures crying out for redemption. The *Gaṅgā* is therefore *Śiva* in another form *śivasvarupiṇī*.[87]

LEGENDS OF BHAGĪGRATHĀ

It is worth considering here that *Bhagīrathā* - although he had communion with divine forces through his severe *tapas* - was, after all, just a man. Not only did he revive the spirits of his ancestors from their ashen remains and make the divine river flow through a sinful world plunged in darkness, he gave hope to the wretched and the falled. Regardless of caste, age, sex, or offence, the sacred river does not turn anyone away from absolution by her waters. Touched by her, they do not have to suffer years of *penance*, make sumptuous offerings of the gods, acquire knowledge of the scriptures, or even secure the mediation of priests. The waters are there for every soul, living or dead. This fact alone makes the story of her descent and the man who made it possible remarkable. But what kind of a character was *Bhagīrathā*, and why was he chosen for this deed in the first place?

---

87 See *Vedavyāsa* Pranita Kasikhanda Calcutta, R K Mission Sevashram 1322 (1915-1916).

The sixty thousand sons of *Sagara* had to be punished for their destructive ways and their excessive hubris. This was why the king of gods, Indra secretly decided to lead their sacrificial white horsed astray. Furious, they laid the earth to waste looking for the seed. When they finally found the horse in Kapila's Ashram, they not only disrupted his mediation and prayers but also insulted and tormented him. The fact that they were smitten and incinerated by the great sage's rage was a fitting punishment. Far from home and deep in the netherworld, they were burned to ashes without a funeral or last rites. Their spirits were denied a final resting place. However, sins in the *Purāṇas* are not merely a function of individual culpability and are not even entirely the poison to one's own *karma*. They are also tied to ancestral deeds. *Sagara's* sons inherited their characteristic flaws.

King *Sagara* was the child born of King *Vāhu* and Queen *Yadavī* in the great clan of *Ikshvāku*. *Vāhu* had another wife who was jealous of *Yadavī* and when *Yadavī* was pregnant, she tried to poison her. By divine grace, she did not die or lose the child. *Vāhu* had many enemies, and they saw this ordeal as an opportune moment to attack him; he had to flee to the forest with his family including his pregnant wife. Because of the action of the poison, *Sāgara*, when he was a fetus, could not see the light of day for a hundred years. Vahu died after many yeas in exile, and *Yadavī* prepared to mount her husband's funerary *pyre*. At this critical moment another great sage, Ourva, appeared and asked her not to throw herself into the fire. *Yadavī* was with child, he beseeched, and an act of self-immolation in this case would surely end thelife of the unborn. Ourva foresaw that *Sāgara* would grow up to be a good king and a formidable warrior, and he would one day avenge his father's death by defeating his enemies. Thus persuaded, *Yadavī* decided not to take her own life and went with Ourva to live in his hermitage, where she eventually gave birth to a boy who had survived poisoning. And thus he was named *Sagara* (sa gara), "one born with pison. *Sagara* was brought up and educated in the āshram. He learned the *Vedas* and studied the arts of combat. He resolved to resolved to recover his father's lost kingdom and vanquished the clans of the *Haihayas, Talajanghas, Yavanas, Śakas*, *Kambojas*, and others.

The segment of the story appears in many sources, including the Bhagavata Purāṇa, the *Brahmā Purāṇa*, the *Padma Purāṇa*, and the *Mahābhārata*. What follows has been narrated before in the context of the *Rāmāyaṇa*, baring some variations. Sagara was unable to father a child and propitiated *Śiva* with prayer and offerings. Śiva promised him progeny from each of his two queens. One would be mother of sixty thousand strong sons, all of whom would eventually perish. The other would give birth to the son who would carry his line. In due course both queens were expecting. *Sumati* gave birth to a beautiful son. The other queen, *Keshinī*, gave birth to a gourd. This sixty thousanhd sons were begotten from these seeds. The *Brahmāvaivarta Purāṇa* states that *Keshinī* gave birth to a ball of flesh, which by the grace of Śiva and the ḅlessing of the *Gaṅgā* was split into sixty thousand parts, each of which became a son.[88]

As they grew up, *Sagara*'s sons became a band of unruly tyrants. The son from the other queen, *Asāmanja*, was different. *Bhagīratha* was the great grandson of *Asāmanja* and the son of *Dilīpa*. All of *Sāgara*'s progeny were cursed from the beginning because of the lingering effects of the poison that had been administered to his mother. Even the lineage that was kept alive by Asamanja almost came to an end with *Dilīpa*, who proved to be impotent and could not father any children. As we shall see, *Dilīpa* was not exactly *Bhagīratha*'s natural father. *Sagara*'s sons and grandsons had been tainted by the poison, and all tried in vain to bring *Gaṅgā* down to earth from the heavens, hoping that she would flood the subterranean realms and the crater that contained the residuum of the sixty thousand sons incinerated during *Kapila's* warth. They all failed except for *Bhagīratha*.

Bhagīrathā's patience is considered exemplary in the Indian mythological repertoire, and his self-imposed penance

88 *Brahmavaivartupurāṇam* p. 105.

and mortifications as an offering to the gods are remembered as exemplary acts of virtue. However, only because of his pure heart did he persuade the river goddess to break forth on the planet, flood the subterranean realm, and then mingle with the ocean. *Bhagīratha* did not carry his ancestor's curse because he was not conveived out of an ordinary union between man and woman. Some of the *Purāṇas* indicate that he was born out of sexual congress between the two queens of King *Dilīpa*. And because *Bhagīratha* was conceived without semen, he did not carry the seed or the curse that his father *Dilīpa* had inherited from his ancestors. *Bhagīratha* was not an offspring who resulted from an ordinary consummation, and this made him spotless and pleasing to the gods.

VERSATILE NARRATIVES

The ubiquity of the Gaṅgā myth in India demonstrates how popular culture digests and regurgitates narratives without breaking down their basic structure. This is evident in Bengali texts on the *Gaṅgā* from eastern India at least from the fourteenth century. They ascribe *Bhagīratha's* birth to a miracle of double maternity. According to scholars who are interested in aspects of feminity and atypical forms of gender identity in medieval India, the Bengali versions of the *Padma Purāṇa* and the *Rāmāyaṇa* stand out in their characterization of the genesis of *Bhagīrathā* as a result of the sexual union of two women. A version of this female - centered story appears in some manuscript versions of the *Padma* that have been found in eastern Bengal.[89] It also appears in detail in *Krittivāsa's* widely popular *Rāmāyaṇa*, written in Bengali, which dates to the late fifteenth century. A similar account appears in *Dvija Mādhab's* compositions extolling the *Gaṅgā*, which appeared almost two hundred years after the writing of Krittivāsa's Ramāyaṇa.

The episode on creatin (*sṛṣṭikhanḍam*) that appears in a popular version of the *Padma Purāṇa* collated by Abdul Karim provides a

---

89 Swargakhanda of *Padmapurāṇa,* Varanasi, Indias Kashiraja Trust, 1972, pp.140-141

detailed account of *Bhagīrathā's* lineage and place in the *Ikshvāku* clan produced legendary kings such as *Māndhātā*, whose name in Sanskrit is synonymous with "antiquity"; King *Hariṣchandra*, famous for his sacrifices and suffering; and also King *Vāhu*, father of *Sagara*, who survived poisoning. *Sagara* became very accomplished and powerful because he grew up in the *Āshram* of Sage Bhargava, who taught him how to use weapons that spouted fire. Later as a king he commanded the greatest horse - sacrifice with a stallion that emerged from the depths of the ocean. This is the same horse that *Indra* stole and brought back to the underworld, and the one that *Sagara's* sons searched for, tearing up the earth. This form of *Bhagīrathā's* genesis is narrated with vivid imagination in Krittivasa's *Rāmāyaṇa*, one of the most widely circulated and recited texts from medieval Bengal.[90] In *Krittivāsa's* rendition, *Bhagīratha's* father, *Dilīpa*, spent 1,000 yeas in severe penance, fasting for long periods and even forgoing water, seeking redemption from the gods for his fallen ancestors. Eventually, *Dilīpa* died without a son to carry on the name of clan and the dynasty. However, his suffering had stirred the conscience of *Śiva*, who came down from his abode in Mount *Kailua* in search of *Dilīpa's* two queens and appeqared in front of them in his original form. He told them, "One of you will conveive from my boon. The queens, surprised to hear this, exclaimed, "But we are widows!" *Śiva* then asked the two women to make love to each other and assured them that they would beget a child from this unusual union. Acquiescing to this request, the two queens bathed and prepared for this ritual. When one of them had become fertile, they made love. Just as *Śiva* had primised, a baby was born in ten months time. However, because the child was begotten without semen, it was nothing but a lump of flesh, with no skeleton. Much distraught at this outsome, the two mothers wept. They could not figure out how to raise this deformed child.

---

90 See Subodh Chandra Majumdar (ed) *Krittivāsa* Rachita *Saṁpurāṇa Rāmāyaṇa*, Calcutta, 1958.

Pūtra kole kore kandena duijona
Heno pūtra bara keno dila trilocana
Asthi nahi, mamsapinḍa colite na pare
Dekhiya hasibe loka sakala samsare[91]

The two sat crying with their son in their lap
Why did the third - dyed - one give such a blessing ?
No bones, a lump of slesh unable to move
The whole world would laugh at it

Despite his disfigurement, the boy survived and grew up in the care of his two mothers. Because he had been born out of the union of two women, he was called *Bhagīratha*. One day the famous sage *Aṣṭabakra* was passing down the street when he saw the young boy. *Aṣṭabakra* was an old man bent in eight places" and moved with much paid and difficulty. Not knowing the boy's history or condition, the sage thought that *Bhagīratha* was mocking his movements. Enraged at this, *Aṣṭabakra* was about to curse and incinerate the boy with his supreme rage (-*brahmāsapa*), when he realized that in fact he had been born with a curse. His rage turning to empathy. *Aṣṭabakra* decided to use his special powers and endow *Bhagīratha* with a skeleton. This is how *Bhagīrathā* survived.

As *Bhagīrathā* grew up, he decided to ask about his father. People would not tell him the truth. They made fun of him and hurled insults. Shamed and humiliated, he pestered his mothers to tell him the true story of his conception. When he found out about his family and his ancestors, a new resolve arose in his heart. He decided that he would bring *Gaṅgā* down to the earth and assuage the sins of his ancestors, whose ashen remains lay near the sanctuary of the great seer *Kapila*. Just as his father had done, *Bhagīratha* sought out of the highest mountains and began to pray to Śiva for help. He disregarded all physical comfort, winter cold, and summer heat. At one point during his austerities, he even submerged himself in water for four months. No one had seen such dedication, such

91 English Translation by the author (Sri Subodh Chandra Majumdar)

painful penance. Eventually, his suffering began to move the great gods *Brahmā* and *Viṣṇu*. As the text indicates, the one holding the *cakra* (*Viṣṇu*) dissolved (*drabarupa hailena nije cakrāpāni*). This idea of "dissolving" out of love for the humble human supplicant is noteworthy, for a makrs the text with an cmotion that is typical of medieval devotion, often described as bhakti, which had begun to flourish in Bengal around this time.

Thus the heavenly Ganṭā, the essence of *Viṣṇu's* dissolving kindness, plunged earthward from *brahmāloka*, the seat of the gods. First she fell on the great mountain *Sumeru*, the highest point on earth, and resided there for twelve years, locked in a dark, vast cavern. There the waters of the river thrashed about, with no place to go,wrapped in blinding darkness. Finally *Gaṅgā* pleaded for release, and asked *Bhagīrathā*, the man who had precipitated her fall, "which way out?" Who could cut through ice and rock and let her waters out of this lofty prison? Gaṅgā asked *Bhagīratha* to ask for Indra, the king of gods, to lend his mascot, the great white elephant *Airāvata*, who would be able to tear up the side of the mountain with his gigantic tusks. The mighty *Airāvata*, lord of elephants, came trumpeting to the rescue. However, bedazzled by the divine beauty of the goddess *Gaṅgā*, the rutting beast desired her. Here, *Krittivāsa's* text takes on a distinctively ribald tone. *Gaṅgā* told the elephant that she would consent to lie with him if he could withstand more than two waves. Blinded by lust, *Indra's* elephant tried to ride the mighty waves of the *Gaṅgā* and nearly drowned. Rescued from the water and duly humbled, *Airavata* cut the great mountain *Sumeru* into four giant sections with his enormous tusks, and the *Gaṅgā* fell into four distinct streams: *Vasu, Bhadra, Shveta*, and *Alkanandā*. Vasu proceeded to flow toward the eastern sea, while the other three rivers tell straight down to earth, then cascaded in three different directions. Having almost drowned, *Airāvata*, exhausted and having fulfilled his task, beat a hasty retreat.

Krittivāsa's version of the Bengali *Rāmāyaṇa* is now a standard text. Looking at this detailed account of *Bhagīratha's* genesis, penance, and the coming down of the *Gaṅgā* to the earth, one can form an idea of how widespread this version of the story had become in eastern India. It sets the stage for other texts in Bengali from this period onward, and the story became even more embellished with details and characters, more patchwork in the fabric of popular imagination surrounding devotion to the *Gaṅgā* and its waters in various forms. Another, more concise text from Bengal, the *Gaṅgāmangala*, composed during the late sixteenth century and attributed spontaneity (*līlā*).[92] In the episode dedicated to Gaṅgā's matrimony with *Śiva*, *Durgāprasad* gives a vivid account of the feminine rituals of rural Bengal (*ṣtrī-acārā*).

Led by *Bhagīrathā*, *Gaṅgā* tumbles out of heaven from *Brahmā's* water pot in three streams: Mandakini in heaven, Bhagavati in the netherworld and Alkanandā on earth. With the help of Indra's elephant, she bursts out of the *Himālayas* and follows *Bhagīratha* through the northern Indian plains. Gaṅgā carefully skirts the holy city of *Kashianḍ* sallies forth toward the ocean. Here Durga Prasad recounts a familiar geography of the major cities of the present day *Gaṅgā* valley: Munger, Bhagalpur, Kahalgaon, Rajmahal, and entering the great Bengal *delta*, Nabadwip, Ambika, Shantipur, and all the way to *Kalighāt* in Kolkata. In the course of his description, Durga Prasad gives vivid details of fairs and markets and the bustling trade of tobacco and betal-but. When she finally arrives near the island of *Sāgara*, Where the cinders of King *Sāgara's* accursed progeny are kept, a great shining chariot emerges from her waters, which bears *Bhagīratha* like a newly anointed king, he is finally able to make an offering (tarpana) on behalf of his forsaken ancestors and deliver them to heaven (*vaikunṭa*), with the help of two hundred thousand golden pots of *Gaṅgā* water.[93]

92 Durga Prasad Mukhopadhayay's *Gaṅgābhakti Tarangini*, Calcutta, 1855, p. 8.

93 Ibid pp. 113-117.

AND ENDURING ICON

Bhagīratha's steadfastness and resolve to bring down the river and propitiate the spirit of his ancestors has been celebrated across many walks of Indian literature. Considered an exemplar of poetic composition, the celebrated *Gaṅgāvataranam* of *Nīlakanṭa* Dikshitar, scholar, poet, and philosopher of seventeenth-century Madurai in Tamil country, on the descent of the Gaṅgā is a composition of eight cantos and is still studied today along with the greatest craftsmen of Sanskrit verse such as *Kālidāsa* and Bhavabhūti. Nilkantha's poem is not just an ode to the river but also a rousing tribute to King *Bhagīrathā*, who donned the loincloth of a holy mendicant (*muniveśa*) and embraced the long and difficult penance that finally disturbed the equanimity of Lord *Brahmā* and caused the mighty river to inundate earth with here resplendent purity.[94] In Nilakantha's story, the celestial river, pleased by *Bhagīrathā's* entreaties, agrees to his request but warns him that her plunge to earth might drown and destroy *Brahmā's* great creation (*jagadanḍamanḍala nimajjayaṅtiva*).[95] In this version of the myth, Gaṅgā enters the mortal realms behind a triumphant *Bhagīrathā*, who is conducted through the crowded streets of the cities in kingly glory *Nīlakanṭa's* description evokes images of royalty that must have been rypical of his time. This is how he describes *Bhagīratha's* swift chariot, with the river making its course by following his path:

> *atha sannnihitam Bhagīratham saritam tamapi tadrathanugam*
> *avalokitumicchatam nrnamatulastatra babhuva sambhramah*[96]
> *And right behind Bhagīratha, the river trailed his chariot*
> *Countless people who wanted to see this were filled with awe*

---

94 Kapil Deogiri (ed) *Gaṅgāvataranam* of Nilakantha Dikshit, Varanasi, 1985, pp 26-27.

95 Ibid p. 26.

96 Ibid p. 75 see also pt. *Kedarnāth* Sastri (ed) The *Gungāvataraṇa* of Nilkantha Diksit, Bombay, 1916, p. 56.

Roughly contemporary no *Nilakanṭa*, another acclaimed figure, *Jagannātha Panditarāja*, a great scholar of linguistics, poetics, aesthetics, and philosophy, wrote a great ode to the Gaṅgā, the *Gaṅgālaharī* (Flow of the Gaṅgā). *Jagannātha* arrived at the Delhi court as a young man from Telengana during the reign of Emperor *Jahaṇgir* and became a court poet. Emperor *Shah Jahān* loved hearing his compositions and granted him the covered title of *Panditarāja*, "king of scholars." *Jagannātha* was exiled because of his connection with the *Mughals*, and also because of his marriage to a Muslim woman of *Shah Jahan's* court. The cantos of the *Gaṅgālaharī* are a testament to *Jagannatha's* poetic virtuosity, but they also include some of the most moving devotional eulogies ever offered to the Gaṅgā. They also suggest a transformation of the figure of the Gaṅgā from a young maiden, a symbol of fecundity and bounty, to a maternal figure of forgiveness and compassion. In *Jagannātha's* imagery, Mother (*janānī*) *Gaṅgā* has forsaken the lotus feet of Viṣṇu and the refuge of *Śiva's* heavenly locks to deliver the fallen (*patitajananiṣtaraṇa*). She is as fair as the autumn moon, seated on a white *Makara* and crowned by the white serpent and lunar crescent; two of her hands hold the earthen pot and the lotus (*kumbhāṁbuja*), and the other two are folded in thegesture of blessing and *abhaya* ("fear not").[97]

These poetic images vary considerably in time and space, which is also a function of localized folk traditions. Examined more closely, however, at least two archetypes seem to emerge that support the overarching icon. One is in elusive and enigmatic figure, resembling the fickle deities of fortune in the Indian tradition. The other is an embodiment of the natural plenty, all - embracing and all - forgiving. The duality is evident in the classic corpus of the *Mahābhārata*, whose natural setting is along the western most part of the Gaṅgā plains. The Gaṅgā makes a number of appearances in the *Mahābhārata* in theguise of both a goddess and a beautiful woman, and in her beguiling form, she becomes an instrument of

97 Pt. Jagannath, Gaṅgālahrī, The flow of Ganges Varanasi, 2007, p. 63.

fate. Take the example of the story of King Mahābhiṣa, who in the company of the gods in heaven chanced upon Gaṅgā naked, and she returned his glance.[98] Watching this unseemly exchange, Brahmā became annoyed and banished Mahābhiṣa to earth. He was reborn as Sāntanu, and King *Pratipa* became his father. At this time Gaṅgā decided to help the eight *Vasus* cursed by the sage Vaśiṣṭa,who had altered their sex and turned them into men. To regain their status as *nymphs*, the *Vasus* asked to be reborn as *Gaṅgā's* own children, because as celestial beings they could not be born in the womb of an ordinary human. They alsoasked their future mother to kill them at birth by drowning, so that their spirits could be released. Gaṅgā agreed to this, but also requested that one of her eight children be allowed to live.

One day, when the devout King *Partipa* of the great *Kuru* clan was enrapt in meditation, at the souorce of the Gaṅgā (*Gaṅgādvāra*), the river assumed the form of a beautiful maiden (*strirupadhārinī*), rose from the water seductively, and sat on King *Partipa's* right thigh to entice him, breaking his concentration. Pratipa asked her what she wanted, and Gaṅgā said that she desired him. Pratipa, however, had taken a vow of abstinence and refused to be moved by lust. He pointed out that *Gaṅgā* was sitting on his right thigh, which was meant for children and daughters-in-law. The wise Pratipa asked her instead to take his son as husband when he came of age. Gaṅgā consented to this, as long as her visit was kept secret and no one questioned her actions. Before he died, *Pratipa* told his son that one day a beautiful woman was going to seek him out, and he must accept her as his wife. And in due course, roaming the banks of the Gaṅgā during a hunting expedition, *Śāntanu* came upon the same exquisite (*parāmam*) woman who had appeared before his father. Smitten by her beauteous form, *Śāntanu* asked her to marry him, thus fulfilling his father's last wishes. Gaṅgā became his wife and was soon with child, and when it was born she promptly drowned it

98 JAB Van Buitenen, The *Mahābhārata* Book I, The Book's of Beginning Chicago, 1973, p. 216.

in the river, exactly as planned. In this way Gaṅgā disposed of the first seven sons, but the eighth time *Śāntanu* intervened. The boy who survived grew up to be the great warrior *Bhīsma*.

These descriptions of the river in human form, an *amphibian*, fickle, voluptuous beauty, who wants to bear the sons of the king only to take their lives by tossing them back into the waters, paint her as a composite figure that straddles the divide between water and earth. The form in which *Pratipa* and his son *Śāntanu* see her is worth remarking: she has a resplendent body and wears a gossamer fabric, shining like lotus-hearted Viṣṇu (padmodarasamaprabha), the goddess *Shrī* incarnate. This invocation of the goddess Shri is significant. *Shrī* and *Bhūmi* are both goddesses of fortune, they have different origins, but they become largely synonymous in the *Upaniṣads*.[99] They are both consorts of *Viṣṇu* and precursors of *Lakṣmi*, and in the *Mahābhārata*, their qualities are re-embodied in thefigure of *Draupadī*, the principal wife of the five *Pāṇḍava* brothers, whose dishonor sows the seeds of war and destruction. *Shrī* as the goddess of prosperity rises from the lotus, shiny and moist, an embodiment of the living verdure, redolent of earth and manure, slime and mud. The litany of references to water and earth bodies suggests that *Gaṅgā* as a deity belongs to a bybrid pantheon of fertility figures tied to the history of the dispersal and assimilation of animistic cults and guardian deities. As we shall see later in this book, they found renewed expression in everyday culture as Jainism and Buddhism redefined the languages and affects of popular piety, contributing to the historical depth and iconic complexity of Gaṅgā as a feminine form, part human, part water.[100]

---

99 Gonda J. Aspects of Eearly Viṣṇuism, Delhi, 1969, pp. 212-213.

100 Sen Sudipta, op. cit. pp. 68-69.

CHAPTER 3

THE GAṄGĀ THROUGH THE AGE OF EMPIRES IN INDIA

The English East India Company succeeded in edging out its European rivals, scuttling French imperial ambitions in India in the wake of the Seven Years' War (1760) and, in capturing Bengal, turning its Nawab into a cipher. The British traders and their Indian agents lodged themselves in the country trade of the interior, drawn into frequent skirmishes with local authorities. After 1765 they began to treat the eastern seaboard as an imperial acquisition, with exclusive rights to the revenues of Bengal, Bihar, and Orissa in return for one annual payment to the *Mughal* ruler in Delhi, increasingly powerless and confined to his palace. They set up custom houses, police posts, and checkpoints across much of these tracts, brought to heel unruly *zamindars*, and secured most of the market places between *Dhaka* and *Varanasi*.

Temples, mosques, hospices, fairs, and markets along the Gaṅgā had always been subject to political struggle between competing regimes. With considerable forethought, *Akbar* decided to erect a massive fort at the confluence of the *Gaṅgā* and the *Yamuna* in

Allahabad. In the eighteenth century, before the British had fully curbed the militancy of local regimes, trading and fighting groups such as the ascetic sanyasis vied for the control of pilgrimages. As the company seized the reins of administration, this volatile landscape began to change once again, not just in the *Bengal delta*, but beyond Mirzapur and Banaras upriver, Europeans, including company factors, had been floating up and down for decades on the Gaṅgā in native budgerows fitted with both oar and sail, and now they were in charge of the river and its valley, which along with the old Grand Trunk Road was home to the annual traffic of more than 25,000 tons of country cargo.

It describes how the Gaṅgā was mapped and reclaimed in the eighteenth century, how the lower Gaṅgā plains and the Bengal delta formed the core of the East India Company's imperial territories in India, and how, after the great uprising of 1857, the valley of the Gaṅgā became a part of village India of the British Raj. It took a long passage of history to pacify the valley and weed out unfriendly landlords, rebellious chiefs, and hostile tribes. Forests were cleared and swamps drained to make way for an unprecedented expansion of villages and land under cultivation, as steamships and railways followed. A consensus seems to be emerging now among environmental historians of India that the British Empire played a unique role in the transformation of the ecological and environmental landscape of the Indian subcontinent, especially in the manner in which it claimed raw materials and resources for its exhara of the global industrial country.[101] The plains of northern India bore the burnt of this upheaval over the course of the nineteenth century. At the same time, in travelogues etchings, and watercolors the image of a picturesque and beatific Ganges flowing through the heart of Britian's proud Indian acquisition took hold of the *Victorian* imperial imagination.

---

101 Kumar Deepak, Damodaran Vinatu and Rohan D'souza, The British empire and Natural World, Environmental encounters in South Asia, New Delhi 2011, pp. 1 to 5.

Merchant - Riders

Sometime during the early years of the sixteenth century, renegade bands of *Portuguese* and *Arakanese* descent began to raid the ports and estuaries of the Bay of Bengal from *Chittagong* in the west to *Satgaon* and *Huglī* on the Gaṅgā in the east. Mukundaram *Chakaṛabarti*, in his memorable verses dedicated to the goddess *Chanḍī*, describing the seaward journey of the legendary merchant Dhanapati Singhala, mentions his fleet passing the country of the *phiringis* (Franks), sailing all night long for the fear of their armadas (*harmada*).[102] It is clear from this description that by the 1530s the *Portuguese* had extended their maritime activities in Bengal and staked their claim on the banks of the lower Gaṅgā *delta*, adding to the menace of pirates.[103] The Bengal sultans were well aware of the fact that these waterways to the ocean were difficult to patrol, which is why *Arakanese* raiders, the dreaded "mags" of the Bengal littoral, had been able to carry on their traffic in local commodities and slaves for centguries.[104] Bengali seafaring vessels traveled with armed mercenaries (paiks) to defend against such sudden raids.[105]

The course of the river *Huglī* had narrowed over the centuries, but descriptions of Bengali poets from the Mughal era suggest a busy traffic of boars and seagoing vessels up and down the distributaries and channels from *Huglī* to the great pilgrimage of *Sagar Island.*[106] These myriad outlets to the Bay of Bengal are marked clearly in Portuguese and *Dutch* navigational charts and the maps of Joao de Barros and Mattheus Van den Broucke. De Barros, in his Decadas da Asia, describes the Sundarbans, or Cape Segogora, recognized by sailors by its distinctive lines of palm - a coastline known to

102 Kalikankana Candi, Dvitiya Bhag (ed) D. Sen C. Bandopadhyay & H. Basu, Kolkata, 1926, p. 669.

103 Chrles Fredrick Darvers the Portugal in India, Being a history of the rise and decline of their Eastern empire, New Delhi, 1984 (1992), vol. I, p. 422.

104 Ghosh, Jamini Mohan, Magh Raider in Bengal, Calcutta, 1960, pp 17-18.

105 Gupta, Tanonash Das, Prachina Bangala Sahitya Katha, Calcutta, 1948, p. 96.

106 Sen, Sudipta, op. cit. p. 303.

Portuguese sailors by the beginning of the sixteenth century C.E. De Barros provides a map along with a description of settlements and markets between the mouth of the *Gaṅgā* and *Chittagong*. The outlets of the Gaṅgā here, he shows, have dissected the land (*toda terra cortada*) into a myriad of unknown and low lying (baixos) islands. A similar account of these labyrinthine creeks and flats is given in the seventeenth-century compendium of Pedro Barreto de Resednde and Antonio Bocarro on *Portuguese* possessions in the Indian Ocean called the Livto das Plantas de Todas as Fortalezas, Cidades c Povoacoes do Estado da India Oriental, still presenting the *Bengal delta* after almost a hundred years as a remote and forbidding place (*extreme lugar*). Here the sea cuts the earth in and endless series of islands and lowlands, and rivers shed their waters into the ocean through many mouths of which two are best known (*mais celebres*): Satgaon and *Chittagong*. By this period these parts of the coast had become the haunts of Arkanese pirates and Portuguese freebooters, along with *Malays, Arabs*, and other advengurers, who from time to time carried off local inhabitants to be sold as slaves and eunuchs. This may have been one of the reasons why large tracts of the *delta* between *Huglī* in the east and the *Chittagong* Hills in the west remained unsettled, covered with swamps and marshes, subject to periodic flooding, and infested with tigers, crocodiles, and other wild beasts. Accounts of early Jesuit travelers such as Pierre du Jarric, from Toulouse, France, who traveled between *Huglī* and *Chittagong* in the late sixteenth century, describe a forbidding terrain of dense vegetation and runny marshes with crocodiles, and tigers with a taste for human flesh that could pursue boats for miles. Father Jarric saw a tigere jump onto a boat with thirty passengers and carry off an African slave from thehold.[107] Such gloomy accounts of the Bengal coastal waters "full of rocks and dangerous shelves" guarding a vast, inhospitable *delta* of "shallows and flats" is shared by many

107 Father Pievre du Jassic, A Missionary Tourism Bengal Tr. from the French and Annotated by the Rivvend A Sauliere Bengal Past and Present vol. 14 no.2, 1907, p. 149.

other travelers and traders, not just Jesuit priests.[108] The letters of Nicholas Pimenta record visitors to *Bengal* from the *Portuguese* settlements in *Goa* and *Cochin*, especially the mission of Francis Fernandes and Dominick Sosa, who was struck by the extent of this expansive wilderness.

Around the time of *Vasco da Gama's* historic voyage to India, the *Portuguese* had already established a string of coastal trading outposts equipped to replenish caravels destined for trade in spices, slaves, and textiles, and other precious cargo across the greater Indian Ocean. Very soon, extensive stretches of the northeastern oceanic rim, including the *Arabian Sea* and the *Bay of Bengal*, would be added to the network of islands and enclaves that made *Portugal* such a formidable amphibious power. This emerging view of the translantic *Indian Ocean* world is evident in contemporary records such as Duarte Pachedo Pereira's handbook Esmeraldo de Situ Orbis, written in 1508, which contains not only vivid descriptions of the West African slave coast but also detailed charts of the navigational distances of Indian ports such as *Calicut* and *Cannanore* and geographical speculations about the country immediately surrounding the mouth of the River Gaṅgā ("India rodeando ha entrada y foz do rio guanje")[109]

Early eighteenth-century accounts begin to take notice of the rapid growth of *Portuguese* settlements in *Chittagong*, now rechristened as Porto Grande distinct from the settlers of the *Huglī* estuary, known as the *Porto Piqueno*. This smaller port lay downriver from the old entrepot of *Satgaon*. M. Caesar Frederick, a Venetian merchant, visited the harbor of Porto Piqueno, sailing along the coast and up the Gaṅgā to a city called Satagan (*Satgaon*), where he saw a long procession of boats. Some had covered a distance of almost 100 miles from the coast, a journey of eighteen hours, and among them were country barks, large bazaars (*Bengali bajra*)

108 Ibid., pp. 3 to 7.

109 Duarte Pacheco and Raphael Eduarano de Azevedo Bato, Esmeraldo de situ orbis, Lisbon, 1892, pp. 10-15.

laden with merchandise, and smaller dingies (*patuas*). He was stuck by the number of makeshift shacks of straw and mud in a nearby depot known as Betor, a clearinghouse for; ships leaving for ports of call farther east. About thirty-five such vessels left Huglī each year during this period carrying rice, cloth, lacquer, and chili peppers.[110] Ralph Fitch, too during his voyage to Bengal, noted the prosperity of Porto Piqueno, which had become the entry point for boats traveling a league inland to Satgaon.[111] Later British accounts of the ruins of Sargaon, with remains of ground wells and tanks found at depths of 15, 20 or even 30 feet, suggest its gradual decline and the rise of *Huglī*.[112]

The Legacy of Albuquereque

The *Vatican* had granted the *Portuguese* leave to seek out prospects in *Persia* and India; and they were among the earliest Europeans to settle along the coastline of *Bengal*. It is important to note that Bengal at this time was largely independent of *Mughal* Delhi, and the sultans did not have a single fleet to challenge the Portuguese in their coastal waters. By the early fifteenth century C.E. the Portuguese had established themselves as the indispensable agents of trade across the Indian Ocean. Small groups of Pordtuguese had also begun to arrive in Bengal from their various strongholds across the Indian Ocean, including the spice-rich *Malabar* coast, *Sri Lanka*, and the islands of *Malacca*. News of the bustling trade and fabulous merchandise of *Bengal*, especially cotton textiles, traveled to *Goa* and the wider *Iberian* world, prompting theexpeditions of Joao de Silverira and Femao Peres de Andrade.

In 1515, following the death of the legendary pioneer of the *Portuguese* seaborne empire. Afonso de *Albuquerque*, the young Lopo Soares de Albergaria was appointed as the new governor of

110 Samuel Purchas and Richard Haklukt, Kakluytus posthums or Purchas his Pilgrimes Vol 10, Glalgow, 1905, pp. 113-114.

111 Ibid., pp. 28-29.

112 Piddington, A letter to the most Noble James Andrew, p. 8.

the Estado da India, and like his predecessor, he gave a wide birth to *Portuguese* casados (trader-settlers) - not just fidalgos (asistocrats) - who sought to expand their commercial operations along the Bengal coast through their own private enterprise. Such casados included not only white (branco) marked settlers, soldiers, and ecclesiastics but, as Bocarro pointed out, an increasing number of native and mixed - blood Christians or casados pretos (blacks).[113] The *Portuguese* crown at this time was also interested in exploring the possibility of trade across the Bay of *Bengal* and *China* and helped finance the voyage of Fernao Peres de Andrade, who reached the coast of China in 1517 and sent an envoy, Joao Coelho, in a ship belonging to a muslim merchant sailing to Chittagong. It is not clear whether the Muslim rulers of the Bengal delta saw the Portuguese as a blessing or a menace, but Joao de Silveira, dispatched by the governor to establish new trading posts in coastal Bengal, did not seem to have succeeded in his mission. There is no doubt that the Portuguese were keen to explore the prospects of coastal and oceanic trade in *Bengal* as they began to send an annual fleed (carreira) of ships. Contemporary Bengali literature, especially the *Mangalkābya* verses, gives us an impression of a bustling world of coastal and oceanic trade in the Bengal *delta* and the presence of *Chinese* and *Burmese* junks (Bengali *janga-dinga*). Common articles of trade included rice, betel-nut, catechu, *camphor*, spices, dried fish, sugarcane, *jute*, earthenware, essential oils, clarified butter, *vermilion, sea salt*, and *textiles*.[114]

The Portuguese, entrenched in the maritime and coastal trade of Goa and Sri Lanka and in command of the sea lanes frequented by spice-laden Moorish vessels connecting *Cambay*, Hormuz, Basra, Sumatra, and the Straits of Malaccaq, were drawn to this burgeoning trade of the Bengal littoral. By the early fifteenth century they had captured *Diu*, south of *Goa*, and made *Sri Lanka* a nominal

---

113 Subrahmanyam, Sanjay, The Portuguese Empire in Asia, A political and Economic History and editors Chichester, U.K., 2012, pp. 233-234.

114 Dasgupta, Tomonash, Prachina Bangala Sahityera Katha, 1948, p. 27-29.

vassal, weighing in with their armadas and troops in a series of merechantile disputes. Trading and fighting on the high seas were kindred operations for contemporary maritime powers, although J.J. Campos, the pioneering historian of the *Portuguese* in Bengal, asserts that commercial exploration and evangelization were the main unpulses behind these early expeditions.[115] Silveira and Joao Coeho both found their way to Chittagong, looking for permission to trade and set up manufactories. The governor of Chittagong had taken exception to *Portuguese* vessels intercepting two cargo ships from Bengal destined for *Cambay*. Coelho's mission fared better than expected in *Chittagong*, but he did not have an official mandate. Matters came to a head after Silveria and his men, running out of supplies, seized a local boat and snatched its cargo of rice - an act for which the Bengal ruler decided to expel them. Fugitives in the coastal waters, *Silveira* and his men were trapped in a long Bengal monsoon, and to avenge this banishment, he set up a temporary blockade of all shipping in the delta.

Despite such mounting mistrust and hostility, the *Portuguese* continued to send their yearly fleet of ships to Bengal. In 1519 the *Turkish* immigrant from *Tirmiz, Alauddin Husain Shah,* who had established himself as the *sultan of Bengal,* passed away and his son *Nusrat Shah* succeeded at the capital of Gauda, where the *Portuguese* sent their first embassy under Antoniode Brito and Diogo Pereira (a private trader from *Cochin*). They too were treated with due suspicion. When Nuno da Cunha (son of Tristan da Cunha, and Atlantic pioneer) became the capitao - general of the Estado da India, he badly wanted to win back the trust of such local rulers. However, to make matters worse, in 1526 just as the *Portuguese* envoy to the Sultan's court, Dom Martim Affoso, and his men were being taken into custory, Pereira seized a ship owned by the Persian merchant *Khwaja Shihabuddin*. Cunha promised to release the ship, and Affonso was finally freed along with his companions in 1529. Affonso's envoy to the court of Bengal, accompanied by gifts such

115 Ibid., pp. 28-29.

as horses and brocades, also included-alas-bottles of rose water taken from the plunder of a Moorish vessel.

Such incidents make it clear that there was never much love lost between the *Portuguese* and the Bengal sultan, who in an act of caprice caprured and killed Cristovao de Mello, nephew of Governor Lopo Vaz de Sampaio, and ten other *Portuguese* men. Joao de Barros, in his account, decries this as a dark day in the annuals of the *Portuguese* in Bengal, when the rest of the survivors, who were wounded and starving, where treated like animals while they were in custody at Hauda. To avenge this nefarious act, a fleet of nine ships was dispatched under Antonio da Silva Menezes, and the *Portuguese* attempted to force *Sultan* Mahmud Shah to release the prisoners who were about to be forcibly dragooned for the campaign against the *Afghan* upstart *Sher Shah*, threatening to annex Bengal. Menezes's men began to kill, plunder, and torch the port of *Chittagong*. They also set up blockade in *Satgaon*. The *Portuguese* eventually made peace with *Sultan Mahmud* and assisted him in delaying *Sher Shah's* advance by cutting off ferries to mountain passes in the north, fighting valiantly alongside *Mahmud's troops* in a against the *Afghans*, he entrusted the customs houses of Satgaon and *Chitagong* to the *Portguese* in recognition of their assistance and bravery. The Afghan interlude in Delhi, however, came to a sudden end with the accidental death of Sher Shah, weakness and disunity in the Afghan ranks under his successors, and the return of the *Mughal* emperor Humayun. In 1579 Pedro Taveres raveled to Emperor *Akbar's* court in Agra and obtained a much-coveted imperial order, or farman, allowing his people to trade free of duty throughout India. Jahangir would renew these rights in the early seventeenth century. By this period, the Estado da India had been firmly established as a major center for the spice trade between Asia and Europe.[116]

From the point of view of *Lisbon*, the coastlines of *Bengal* and *Arakan* remained distant backwaters of the far-flung Portuguese seaborne empire, places where the Estado da India could never

---

116 Donald F. Lach, Asia in the making of Europe vol. 2, Chicago, 1978, p.11.

exercise adequate control over informal and clandestine networks of trade. These places were not usually inhabited by honorable fidalgos. Recruits who worked the galleys of the *Portuguese* armadas often came from among the poorest sections of the empire and many were prisoners of war or ex-convicts.[117] Resende and Bocarro's Livro das Plantas, while strenuously affirming the fidelity of the Portuguese scattered across the various forts and settlements of the Bay of Bengal to the Estado and the crown, notes nevertheless that the filhos of *Portugal* in the various forts and settlements (*bandies*) were often beyond the reach of the *viceroy's* writ. In such parts, remote from the home country (partes tao remotas de Portugal) and in a state of constant warfare (sempre em continue as guerras), it was easy to disobey the authority of thye crown.[118] Crews and *musketeers* were poorly paid, and many who went to India never came back. The descendants of the *Portuguese* who settled in these parts, Resende and Bocarro inveighed, were of common stock and lacking in self-esteem and honor. They engaged in coastal traffic, were drawn into local political intrigue, and enlisted in rival armies. They also ended up marrying local women and leaving behind *progeny* of mixed blood.[119] Father Pierre du Jarric of Toulouse, in his account of the Jesuit missions in Bengal undertaken in 1598, noted the extensive peuplade (settlement) of *Portuguese* along the River *Huglī* and their church dedicated to St. Mary, frequented by native Christians and *Portuguese* sailors who dedicated foresails of their ships to her for good luck. While in *Huglī*, the fathers also received an appeal from the *Portuguese* Christians of *Satgaon*, who had lost their priest and could not hold Mass. Du Jarric notes that these denizens of the interior were in a state of "great discord and dissention," having long settled down with local women and at the

117 Mathew, K.M. History of Portuguese navigation in India 1497-1600, New Delhi in 1988, p. 139.

118 Rescenda and Bocarro, Livro das plantas, pp. 7-9.

119 E J Brill, The Social world of Ayuthaya 1640 - 1720, Liden Netherland, Boston, 2011, pp. 16-17.

head of large families, attended by slaves and native servants. The Jesuit fathers persuaded many of these women to enter into lawful Christian marriages and gladly baptized them and their children.

The *Portuguese* of the Bengal littoral and their mixed - blood, Christianized, Portuguese - speaking descendants have not been treated kindly in the account of *Chittagong* and *Satgaon*, described them as castoffs who teamed up with the rogue Arakanese to set up an extensive traffic in slave boys and eunuchs. Sebastien Manrique, the noted traveler who visited Bengal and *Arakan* during the 1630s, observed that they were seen by local people primarily as raiders and slavers and noted how he and other priests in his entourage alarmed the natives, who mistook them for soldiers who had come to capture and sell their young.[120]

The Age of Merchantile Rivalry

Not with standing their depredations, the *Portuguese* had opened up the coastal trade of Bengal to the markets of the greater Indian Ocean. Sandalwood, prized as a ritual commodity among Hindus, came by *Portuguese* vessels from the distant islands of *Malacca*, *Sumatra, Borneo,* and *Timor*, as did brocade, velvet, satin, and damask from the *Persian Gulf.* Bengali and Coromandel raffetas and muslin made their way to new European markets. Cinnamon and *pepper* from *Sri Lanka* and the *Malabar Coast,* as well as red chili peppers from the New World, became part of the established culinary repertoire, Sugar, silk, woodwork, and boxes came from China. *Pearls, conches*, and sea shells came on *Portuguese* caravels plying through the Maldives.

Emperor *Akbar's* investiture of 1579 supporting Jesuits and Iberian merchants gave further legitimacy to the *Portuguese* settlements of the lower *Gaṅgā delta*. A visible reminder of this history is the present-day Basilica of the Holy Rosary, or the Banded Church, overlooking the River *Huglī*, which is perhaps the most significant *Portuguese* monument in Bengal - a symbol of pious

120 Sebastiao, Manique, Interario desebastiao Marriaque Lisbon, 1946. p. 45.

Augustinian resolve to uphold the faith in this distant corner of the Estado da India, administered through the dioceses of *Cochin* and *Saint Thome*, *Huglī* was roughly 40 miles downstream from the *Mughal garrison* of *Rajmahal*. Kafi Khan, following the account of Abdul Hamid Lahori, provides a colorful account of the outbreak of hostilities between the *Portuguese* and the *Mughals*.[121] Emperor *Shah Jahan* had received word that the firings had erected a fort in *Huglī* with lofty towers and walls, amassed cannons and muskets, and built an imposing church where they displayed their gaudy idols.[122] They were reported to oppress travelers and to use their leave for trade to run a lucrative monopoly in tobacco. They were also suspected of converting native orphans to Christianity and trading in slaves. *Shah Jahan* dispatched *Kasim Khan* at the head of a large army and a fleet that made a surprising appearance on the *Huglī*. *Bandel* was attacked in June 1632, and after a siege of about three months it fell to the Mughal forces. The old church was destroyed, and the *Augustinian* fathers who survived were captured and taken to Agra. One of them. Father De Cruz regained the favor of *Shah Jahan* and obtained permission to rebuild the *Banded Church*, which in subsequent the veil of the blessed *Virgin Mary*.[123]

Fast the native population of Bengal the Portuguese were the archetype of the har wearing, musket toting brash European overseas traders Seatered along remote outposts of the *Mughal Empire* they are described by contemporary court chroniclers such as *Abdul Hamid Lahori* as msolent troublemakers rather than a direct political threat, committing acts unbecoming of their station as traders exacting unjust duties from boats that passed their factories, stifling the commerce of *Satgaon*, trafficking in poor children, and consorting with the *Arakanese* pirates. Just like on the west coast of *Africa*, the

121 Kati Kahn's account in DG Crewlord, A brief history of Hughli District, Calcutta 1902, pp. 7-8.

122 Campos, History of the Partquese in Bengal, p. 229.

123 Rev. H. Hosten, Thrudays at the Bandel Convent in 1920, Bengal Past and Present, vol. 26, no. 1, 1923, p. 71.

Portuguese of the *Bengal delta* were feared as musketeers, pirates, slavers, and ruthless mercenaries. They infiltrated the coastal trade and purchased leases for the collection of tolls and duties especially from salt and tobacco, in *Satgaon, Hijli, Chittagong, Sandip* and *Sripur*. Many were involved in the trade between Bengal the Coromandel Coast, and part of Southeast Asia, including *Sumatra* and *Malacca*. People of mixed *Portuguese* and Arakanese extraction frequented the slave markets of contemporary Hijli and Tamluk. Others, marked by their distinctive hats (topas), were people of mixed Portuguese descent who joined the ranks of mercenaries known as the Topasses. The Bengali word *kintal*, denoting people of mixed Indian and *Portuguese* blood (Luso-Indians), is derived from quintal, the Portuguese word for a garden house. Not only did a population of mixed-blood Eurasians emerge from the Portuguese presence, but Portuguese soon became the most common European tongue and through regional variations, the lingua franca of the trading world of the Indian Ocean littoral. *Portuguese* - speaking Luso - Indians held positions of trust as merchantile brokers and keepers of ledgers.

The *Portuguese* grasp on the trade of the *Bengal delta* did not go unchallenged. John Huyghen von Linschoten, a Dutchman who visited in Goa during 1583-1589, took careful notes on the state of Portuguese settlements in India. His Itinerario, translated into several European languages, quickly became a guide for all aspiring European traders and adventurers, because it spoke plainly of the great and rich provinces of *Mughal India*, while noting its poorly defended cities and the weakening hold of the *Spanish - Portuguese* crown over its far - flung outposts. A similarly lavish picture was also circulated through the account of *Ralph* Fitch from England, who had the opportunity to visit Emperor *Akbar's durbar* in 1591. Using Linschoten's charts a *Dutch* fleet left for the Indies under Cornelis Houtman, circumnavigating the *Cape of Good Hope* in 1595 and sailing up to western *Java*. Houtman returned without much to show in his cargo and having lost about two thirds of his original crew, but he had succeeded in sealing a treaty with the king of Bantam, which would soon open up the Straits of Malacca and the Indonesian *archipelago* to *Dutch* oceanic trade. In 1598 five more Dutch squadrons set sail for the East Indies, leading to the triumphal return of naval officer Jacob Corneliszoon van Neck who had pioneered the exploration of *Madagascar* and *Bantam*. The *Dutch* now began to threaten the *Portuguese* sea lanes of the Indian Ocean, blockading *Mauritius* for a period of thirteen years, supplanting the spice trade in *Malacca*, setting up factories and garrisons in *Java* and *Sumatra*, and establishing precedence along the sea lanes of the Far East and the Pacific. In 1597 they had founded the Society for Trade to Distant Countries, which was followed by the establishment of the Dutch East India Company (Verenigde Oostindische Compagnic) in 1602 *Dutch* ships and factories became a common sight along the lower course of the *Huglī* and the coastal waters of the bay. The *Dutch* would soon become the most formidable sea power on the open ocean. They expelled the English from the Indonesian archipelago after the slaugher of *Amboina* in 1623 - a piece of infamy that would live long in the annals of English naval history. After an extended maritime conflict ending with the Battle of *Malacca* (1641), they finally succeeded in edging out the *Portuguese* from the Straits of *Malacca*.[124]

After their expulsion from *Huglī* the *Portuguese* had begun to settle in *Chinsura*, farther down the *Huglī* River, in 1632.[125] Francois Bernier, the French physician from Anjou who visited Mughal India and Bengal in 1665-1666, noted extensive Dutch settlements across the *Bengal delta*. Bernier found that *Bengal* was the great emporium of cotton and silk textiles not only for the *Mughal Empire* but for many of the trading nations of Europe, led by the *Dutch*. "I have been sometimes amazed by the vast quantity of cotton cloths, of

124 Christian, J. Koot, Empire at the periphery British Colonists Anglo-Dutch trade and the development of the British Atlantic 1621 - 1713, New York 2011, pp. 105-106.

125 Yules Henry led, The diary of William Headques, London, 1888, p. 233.

every sort, fine and coarse, white and coloured, which the Hollanders alone export to different places, especially to *Japan* and *Europe*," he wrote.[126] He also gave a description of the Dutch silk factory at *Kasimbazar*, near the capital of the *Bengal* Nawabs, *Murshidabad*, which seems to have employed close to eight hundred native artisans and weavers during this time. Chinsura and the nearby village of *Barangar* on the eastern bank of the *Huglī* also attracted the Dutch. Diaries of the English factor Streynsham Master reveal that the *Dutch* had gained an upper hand in the riverine and oceanic trade of Bengal at this time, dealing in saltpeter, muslins (known also as malmal), taffetas, *ginghams*, and raw silk.[127] The *Dutch* built warehouses to protect silk textiles from humidity and exposure and looms for silk weavers.[128] Their ships could navigate the treacherous sandbanks and shoals of the Gaṅgā better than others.[129]

Alexander Hamilton, in his account of *Bengal*, describes the sprawling houses and gardens of the factors of *Chinsura*, fitted with balustrades and pavilions. Many had Moorish - style terraces with floors of pulverized red stone and walls plastered with lime. There were similar establishments at *Kasimbazar* and at *Malda*, a small town conveniently located at a branch of the Gaṅgā. Malda was a place of "great resort" for weavers, dyers, and dealers of cloth that arrived from all parts of the country, providing for the European factors located as far away as Agra and Gujarat, and also agents dispatched by the merchants of *Banaras*. By the mid-eighteenth century, the *Dutch* ran factories at all the major centers of trade and commerce in Gangetic Bihar and Bengal.[130] Not only did they dominate the trade in bullion from Europe, *Dutch* ships carried tea, porcelain, and finished and raw silk from China: lacquered ware and

126 Bernier, Travels in the Mughal Empire, p. 439.

127 Straynshaam Master, Diaries 1675-1680, vol. II, London, 1911, p. 83.

128 Barnier, Travel in the Mughal empire, p. 365.

129 Ibid., p. 310.

130 Dutta Kalikinker, the Duton in Bengal and Bihar 1740 - 1825 AD, Delhi, 1968, p 1-2.

gold dust from Japan: cloves from *Malacca*: nutmeg and *mace* from *Banda Aceh:* pepper and opium from Sulawest; textiles, indigo, and diamonds from the Bengal delta; calicoes, muslins, cotton, and flax from the *Coromandel* Coast; and shellac, rosewood, saltpeter, and dyes and cinnamon from *Sri Lanka*.[131]

Huglī flourished for a long time as the hub of European trade in the lower *Gaṅgā delta*, with the English, *French, Danes*, and *Dutch* having carved out their respective enclaves in Calcutta, *Chandernagore*, *Serampore*, and *Chinsura. Europeans* became familiar figures in the markets and towns of *Bengal*, typically described as "*hat-wearers*" (*kula-poshan*) in *Persian* accounts. Poet *Bharatchandra*, in his ballad *Bidyasundara*, which is a section of his celebrated composition *Annadamangala* written in the early eighteenth century, mentions hated European mercenaries (Bengal Kolaposa) including Englishmen. Dutchmen (*olandaja*), Frenchmen (farasa), Danes (dinemara), and Germans (*elemana*).[132] While *Aurangzeb* reigned in Delhi, and Bengal was in the hands of his able deputy *Shaista Khan*, the European companies did not dare indulge in any armed conflict. The early company pioneer and Madras agent *Streynsham* Master noted in his aforementioned diary that the English too refrained from raising forts and garrisons, seeking instead the goodwill of the nawab of Bengal and his magistrates.[133] The rivalry between the *Dutch*, English, *French*, and *Danes*, however, was difficult to contain as they fought over markets, weavers, brokers, credit, currency and also bids to obtain favorable grants from the Indian powers in exchange of gifts and embassies. "*Bengal* abounds with every necessary of life," *Bernier* noted in his travels. This abundance had lured so many *Portuguese* and their half-caste progeny to the banks of the *Huglī* River. Jesuits and Augustinians vied with *Dutch* Calvinists and English Protestants for merchandise

131 Grose John Henry & John Carmichael, A Voyage to the East Indian London, 1772, p. 306.

132 Bhattacharya, Bharatachandreva Granthvali Kolkata, 1997, p. 13.

133 Master Dianies, Vol. 2, p. 68.

and profit. There were close to nine thousand Christians in *Huglī* alone, and perhaps more than twenty-five thousand in Bengal during the late seventeenth century. Bernier recorded a common saying among Europeans who resorted to Bengal that the country had "a hundred gates open for entrance, but not one for departure. For nearly two hundred years the burgeoning commercial world of the lower Gaṅgā delta assimilated European newcomers into its extensive networks of trade and exchange, absorbing the influx of New World sliver in exchange of manufactured goods. This part of the East Indies was, as one contemporary put in, a "*bottomless pit* for bullion." The tide turned in the eighteenth century, when the French and the English, through their respective trading companies, began to intervene directly in Indian regional politics and local military conflict to hedge their imperial rivalry.

Duties levied on inland trade had always been a bone of contention between the Indian regional powers and the Europeans. This was particularly true in *Bengal*, where, during the heyday of *Mughal rule*, the nawabs of Bengal exacted duties from all merchants. Indian or European, not only at the major custom houses such as *Sultanganj* in *Patna. Pachottera* in *Murshidabad*, or *Bakhshbandar* in *Huglī*, but also at a myriad of smaller posts and toll houses along rivers and roads of the countryside Grand *firmans* of the *Mughal emperor*, which gave a general leave to European companies for their overseas trade, did not guarantee exemption from all local duties and tolls. At *Huglī* the English East India Company paid a handsome annual tribute (*peshkash*) of 3,000 rupees to trade free of added duties, while the *Danes*, the *Dutch*, and the French paid 2.5 percent on their total invoices. The Nawab's customs officials and clerks furnished inventories (*ravanas*) of each boatload of goods carried up and down the Gaṅgā and issued handwritten clearances (*dastaks*) inspected at smaller toll posts at crossings and ferries. The post (*chauki*) of Jaldanga, situated between the *Dutch* factory of *Chinsura* and the French factory of *Chandernagore*, was set up to stop boats trying to pass under one flag to evade these duties.

A contemporary chronicler, *Munshi Salimullah*, noted that while *Murshid Quli Khan*, the nawab of Bengal, was thankful that his province benefited handsomely from duties levied on the profits of European trading companies and did not wish to impose added exactions on their overseas ventures, he also wanted to make sure that they did not set up forts, bastions and trenches. This was one of the reasons why Job Charnock, former head of the *Kasimbazar* factory who had also served as a factor in *Patna*, sought a remote site for a fortified settlement for the British farther downriver toward the tidal mouth of the *Huglī*.[134]

He would eventually settle for the brackish, low-lying marshes of *Sutanati, Gobindapur*, and *Kalikata*, where he signed a lease with the family of *Sabarna Chaudhuri,* local *zamindars*, for a string of village that would eventually grow into the city of Calcutta, destined as the capital of the British Empire in the East, Alexander Hamilton, who was part of the early English settlement between 1688 and 1723, notes in his account that *Charnock* "could not have chosen a more unhealthful place" because of the proximity of the great saltwater lake to the northeast of the English colony that overflowed after each monsoon, exuding what was then believed to be miasmal vapors afficting local inhabitants with fevers and agues and taking a hefty mortal toil every year.[135] Large tracts of tiger-infestd forest were cut down for the building of *Fort William* and the *esplanade*, and over time, the "*straggling villages*" of *Chowringhee* were converted into a bustling thoroughfare for carriages, lined with elegant brick and whitewashed mansions, and jungles were cleared between the fort and the native settlement of *Chitpur*. However, contrary to *Rudyard Kipling's* niggling epither for Calcutta as a city "*chance-directed*, chance - erected, laid and built on the silt," the site for the fort and settlement of Calcutta was chosen carefully.

134 Wilson, C.R. The Early Annals of the English in Bengal, London, 1895. p. 142.

135 Kipling R.A. Tale of Two cities in works of Rudyard Kipling, New York, 1909, p. 284.

It was defended to the west by a tortuous and deep stretch of the river that was difficult to ford with large armies: it was near multiple outlets to the Bay of Bengal; and *Sutanati* was a burgeoning market for thread, cotton yarn, and textiles. The defenses of *Fort William* were intended for strategic and military protection, not just from the corrupt and rapacious native officers of custom but from rival European companies, especially the French and the *Dutch*. In 1717, the British sent an embassy to the mughal court under *John Surman*; it returned in triumph with a new and extensive farman under the seal of Emperor *Farruksiyar* for trade free of duty. Shielded by this new document, the British pressed their advantage in Bengal during a period when the *Mughal Empire* had been considerably weakened by succession struggles, disloyal nobles, palace coups, and peasant rebellions. During these politically fraught times, many provinces, such as *Bengal* and *Awadh*, while remaining nominally loyal to Delhi, began to exert a far greater degree of autonomy in their internal affairs. While this created an uncertain climate for trade, it also offered new opportunities for the company, its officials, and their dependents.

The *East India Company* was a chartered, joint-stock corporation. The Scottish theorist of political economy *Adam Smith* disparaged it famously as a despotic and oppressive monopoly protected by parliamentary flat. It was controlled by a small group of affluent merchants who served on an exclusive court of directors, whose annual meetings, according to the British prime minister William Pitt the Elder, were run like "little parliaments." While it commanded the major sea lanes and shipping to India and its vast profits generated an average return of around 8 percent for its major shareholders, it did not pay its factors, ensigns, and cadets much in terms of salary. Instead, company servants in India were indirectly rewarded by the lucrative deals in inland or country trade. Private trade yielded high margins of profit, as employees were able to conduct business transactions free of local duties along with those of the company, claiming protection undere the Mughal permission against which the chiefs of English factories could issue handwritten passes (*dastaks*). Armed with such licenses, they outbid local traders and merchants in the traffic of commodities such as salt, betel-nut, and tobacco. Later, the court of directors of the company would acknowledge that the letter of *Mughal emperor* was intended exclusively for the trade of the company and not for the enrichment of individual members who had been for years conducting an illegal trade, profiting from a spurious claim, occasionally supported by violence.[136] Many of these items of everyday use, such as salt, *saltpeter, tobacco, betel leaves,* and betel nut were seen as prestige goods coveted by local merchants, and trading in them required a special favor or dispensation from the *Bengal nawab*. The English intrusion into inland trade was particularly irksome to the deputies and officials of the nawab, as well as *local zamindars* and *landlords*, and it led to repeated conflicts over the passage and examination of boats laden with *East India Company* merchandise plying up and down the River *Gaṅgā*. Boats passing under company papers (*dastaks*) were subject to attach and looting, which is why they often carried armed retainers and muskets.[137] The news of such outbreaks and the increasing militancy of the English worried the Bengal nawabs, and the lengths to which the company was prepared to go to defend their trade threatened to infringe the accepted hierarchy of ruler and merchant in late *Mughal Bengal*. Nawab *Alivardi Khan,* who supported the English trade, reportedly asked why their merchants needed a fort and an army.[138] In 1756, when Alivardi passed away, his young grand son, Siraj-ud-daulah, took charge. Accusing the company of having violated the terms of trade and sheltering fugitives, he ransacked the English factory and settlement in *Kasimbazar*, ordering *Roger Drake*, the governor of Calcutta, to bring down all fortifications. When this was refused,

136 Sen Sudipta Conquest of Market places, p. 110.

137 Sen Sudipta, Empire of free Trade Philadelpnia, 1998, pp. 82-83.

138 Sarkar, J.N. & R.C. Dutt (eds) The History of Bengal, Vol. IV, Dacca, 1943-1948, p. 452.

the nawab marched into the city. *Fort William* had a small garrison of artillerymen and not enough supply to last a siege, and Drake decided to abandon his post and seek shelter in sloops off the coast, leaving its inhabitants to the mercy of the invaders. Siraj stormed the fort and took the garrison, allegedly throwing 146 captives into an ill-ventilated, small cell-which now lives in infamy as the *Black Hole of Calcutta* - where apparently all but 23 perished, according to the eyewitness account of surgeon *John Holwell*. The veracity of this event, which *Karl Marx* once called a "*sham scandal*" invented by the "English hypocrites," has been questioned by many historians, but it gained quick and widespread notoriety as clear evidence of the barbaric perfidy typical of Oriental despots.[139] The incident also stoked the outrage of a young Robert Clive, kept away at *Fort St. David* in the south, who wrote to the directors in London of the loss of the city having caused the "greatest mortifications to the Company and the most barbarous and cruel circumstances to the poor inhabitants.[140]

Clive promised to recover Calcutta and its losses and restore its former rights and privileges, as he left for Bengal with five armed ships from the Royal Navy under the command of Admiral *Charles Watson*. What followed is one of the most well-known chapters in the history of the *British Empire* in India: Fort William was recaptured. General *Mir Jafar* was induced to deseret the nawab's army with the promise that the British would install him as the new ruler, and *Bengal* fell to the British at the battle of *Plassey* - fought near the shady banks of the *Gaṅgā* in 1757. The *East India Company's* military success in *Bengal* and its creation of a string of puppet nawabs on the throne of *Murshidabad* in exchange for unprecedented sums of money was not just a great victory and a terrific windfall that gave the company the keys to the richest province of the *Mughal Empire*, but a decisive punctuation to the extended Indian theater of the European wars that lasted from 1744 to 1763, which put the

---

139 Karl Marx, Notes on Indian History Moscow, 1947, p. 68.

140 Malcoin John, The Like of Rolest Lord Clive, London, 1836, p. 143.

Dutch and the French competition to rest. More than textiles, indigo, or opium, the control of the lower Gaṅgā delta enabled the English to edge out the *Dutch* and the French and secure a monopoly over a much - coveted substance in Europe - potassium nitrate, found in its natural state as saltpeter - a crystal that is produced in soil from the action of bacteria on animal droppings and urine. Along with *carbon* and *sulphur, saltpeter* was an essential element in the manufacture of gunpowder. The environs of Calcutta produced copious quantities of high-quality saltpeter, processed by an entire caste of indigenous saltpeter harvesters known as *Nuniyas*. After they conquered Bengal, Britain would control almost 70 percent of the world's production of *saltpeter*.[141]

The Prize of Bengal

European trading settlements in thelower *Gaṅgā delta* always vied for favor and advantage at the courts of Bengal and Delhi, but they also acted in common interest, rooting out interlopers who tried to claim a share of the trade in contravention of established monopolies and rights. This fragile neutrality fell apart during the outbreak of the War of Austrian Succession in Europe (1740-1748), a tortuous conflict over the *Austro-Hungarian* Empire's claim over Silesia that upended the old alliances between the European powers, pitting the English against Austria and France. The 1748 Treaty of Aix-*la-Chapelle* could not prevent the drift toward further conflict that spilled over into the French and Indian Wars in North America and the *Anglo-French* hostilities that engulfed Bengal and the Carnatic. The East India Company appealed for support from the Royal Navy, whose warships began to frequent Indian waters by 1745 alongside those of the French national fleet. Naval skirmishes took place near the Coromandel Coast, where the English settlement of Fort St. George in Madras was less than 90 miles from the French stronghold in Pondicherry. The Dutch gardens and factories at Chinsura. J. Huygens, the director of the Dutch settlement, wrote to the English

141 Cressy, David, Sultpeter: The Mother of Gunpowde, Oxford, 2013, p. 147.

in Calcutta that the French by this act had broken the "neutrality of the Ganges."[142] Rival trading companies were gearing up for armed conflict fortifying factories, conscripting native mercenaries into standing armies and stockpiling muskets and cannops. This looming threat of war and the political uncertainty in *Bengal* also contributed to the military confrontation that took place between the company and the nawab of Bengal.

In southern India the French outrivaled the British in creating a network of alliances with new and upstart regimes that had reared their heads after the decline of *Mughal* power: the *Nizam of Hyderabad*, the *Maratha* ruling houses the kings of *Mysore*, and the nawabs of *Arcot* and the *Carnatic*. English troops stationed at Madras were critically outnumbered in Pondicherry. Joseph Francois *Dupleix*, son of former director of the French Campagine des Indes, was the chief architect of the French empire in India. He took charge of the struggling factory of *Chandernagore*, put it on a profitable footing, revived the fortunes of the settlement, and became the governor of *Pondicherry* in 1741. Political turmoil in the *Carnatic* gave an opportunity for the French to attack Madras, which they took in 1746, burning down several English factories. A truce was declared in 1748 with the Peace of *Aachen*, and the French gave Madras back to the British, *Dupleix* wanted to establish himself as the undisputed nawab of the *Carnatic*, vehemently opposed by "the *Company's* Nawab," *Mahammad Ali Wallajah* of *Arcot*, who was propped up by the British. French political affairs in India, however, became very chaotic because of the rivalry and quarrel between Duoleix and *Bertrand* - Francois Mahe de La Bourdonnais, a commander in the French navy and the former governor of *Mascarenes*. When La Bourdonnais's fleet was ruined in a major storm. *Dupleix* refused to render help, and he was taken prisoner by the British, who sent him in ignominy to *Paris* for trial. He was consigned to the *Bastille* in 1749, which was banishment that broke his health, and he died

142 James Long Sateston from unpublished records of government from years 1748-1767, Calcutta, 1819, pp. 15-16.

within two years of his acquirtal. *Dupleix* also tell afoul of the members of the *French court* for his *flamboyant* lifestyle and the huge debts he incurred in setting up the French as an Indian power. His recall and replacement by the more prosaic Charlesw Godeheu stymied the French political designs in India, clearing the path for *Clive* and the English.

During the siege of Calcutta the French were allied with the nawab of Bengal: they plied him with 250 chesis of gunpowder and did not help the English who were under attack. While the English company gained power in Bengal the French Compagine des Indes wielded power in the *Deccan*. In June 1758, French troops, under the command of the *Irish* - born Comte de Lally, attacked and burned down the English outpost of Fort St. David, followed by an unsuccessful siege of Madras, British troops from Bengal engaged the *French* forces in *Hyderabad* under the command of *Marquis de Bussy*. By January 1760, the British general Eyre Coote defeated de Lally and took Bussy prisoner in a skirmish that has made its way into the annals of British conquests in India as the short but significant battle of *Wandiwash. Pondicherry* fell to the British in 1761, spelling the end of French imperial prospects in India.

In 1749 William Forth, the Dutch political agent at *Chinsura*, attempted to form an alliance with the newly installed ruler Nawab Mir Jafar, promising to procure ships and reinforcements from Batavia and help him expel the British from Bengal. It is doubtful that the nawab was serious, but a *Dutch* vessel with *Malayan* soldiers appeared at the mouth of the Huglī, which *Clive* and the English promptly intercepted.[143] The *Dutch* pretended that the vessel was bound for the south and had bocked near *Huglī* to avoid *monsoon* squalls, but their designs became clear in October 1759, when seven more warships arrived. The provocation was defused by a timely trade deal offered by *Clive*, but *Holland* remained a thorn in the side of the English in Bengal, helping the nawab increase his troops

143 Malleson, GB, The Decisive Battler of Indiafrom 1746-1849, London, W.H. Allen, 1853, pp. 112-113.

in *Patna* and *Kasimbazar* with seven hundred European and eight hundred crack *Malayan* mercenaries. Matters soon came to a head when the English began to conduct searches and seizures of *Dutch* vessels. In the naval battle that took place at the mouth of the *Huglī*, seven Dutch ships were destroyed and over a hundred *Dutchmen* were killed or wounded. The British seized *Dutch* factories in *Baranagar* and *Chandernagore* and drove the Dutch back to *Chinsura*. A renewed conflict ensued on land. *Colonel Francis Forde* engaged the Dutch forces fought back valiantly, but they did not have adequate artillery support. In a quick, bloody, and decisive battle that took only half an hour. 120 Europeans and 200 Malay soldiers were killed across a ditch used as a line of defense, with *Dutch* officers and 350 European soldiers taken as prisoners.[144] The Dutch debacle at this lesser-known but important battle of *Bedarrah*, in effect, ended Dutch territorial ambitions in Bengal and the Indian subcontinent.

Despite the end of the French and the *Dutch* threats, the restoration of Calcutta, the deposition and murder of *Nawab Siraj-ud-daulah,* and the setting up of *Mir Jafar* on the throne of Bengal, political affairs of the British in thelower Gaṅgā valley were far from settled. The *East India Company* had to secure its factories and weaving districts of *Murshidabad*, *Patna, Dhaka, Lakshmipur,* and *Balasore*, as well as the safety of its goods passing up and down the markets and riverside landings (*ghats*) in the west from disgruntled and hostile elements in the nawab's administration, *zamindars*, and rural chieftains. At least three uprisings against Mir Jafar, in *Midnapore, Purnea* and *Bihar*, were put down with the help of company troops. The assassination of the *Mughal emperor Alamgir II* and the usurpation of power by his minister, threatening to march on the English settlements in the east, did not assuage English fears. In ;this climate of intrigue and uncertainty. *Clive's* replacement as governor - general of Benga, Henry *Vansittart*, decided to remove

144 Broome, Arthur, History of rice and progress of the Bengal Army, vol. I Calcutta, 1850, p. 270.

Mir Jafar and replace him on the throne of Bengal with his son-in-law, *Mir Qasim*, who in exchange for a handsome subsidy ceded the provinces of *Midnapore*, *Burdwan*, and *Chittagong* to the Company.

Mir Jafar, installed in 1757 by *Robert Clive* as the first "puppet" nawab, had turned out to be not only corrupt but feeble and ineffective. *Mir Qasim*, on the other hand, was capable, ambitious, and willful. Rather than being a tool in the hands of company officials, he sought to pursue his own political interests. Unlike the traditional nawabs of Bengal, he did not attempt to reconstitute dynastic rule in *Murshidabad.* Instead, he worked tirelessly to restore the fiscal solvency of his provinces. He did not hesitate to exercise a measure of coercion to realize arrears in rent from the largest estates. While he agreed to meet increasing financial burdens placed on him by the company, he also began to petition company officials about the interference of English factors and their Indian agents in the internal trade and local markets of *Bengal, Bihar*, and *Orissa*. One of the main items in contention was the trade in salt, a lucrative commodity that yielded considerable duties and tolls for the *nawab's treasury.*[145] Along with salt, company servants as private trades had infiltrated the networks of trade in *saltpeter, tobacco, betel-nut,* and *opium*, where they wielded the handwritten *dastaks*, or passes, to ply their goods free of duty. They also abused this authority in local bazaars buying goods below market prices and selling them for high profit, *Clive*, who would later set up a society of traders to oversee the manufacture and trade of salt, acknowledged that the private investment of company factors was deeply resented by local traders and rural landlords, and an enormous number of boats and mercenaries had to be maintained to protect the trade of salt along the Gaṅgā.

The abuse of internal trade by the factors and agents of the company remained one of the key bones of contention between Calcutta and *Murshidabad*, straining the alliance between *Mir Qasim* and the company. As Clive discovered during his second visit to

145 Sen Sudipta, Conquest of Market places, p. 115.

Bengal, the *tyranny* and oppression of private traders had thrown the entire internal commerce of the country into *chaos*. Brandishing the *dastaks* and company standards, European traders and their agents along with armed militias roamed the manufactories, markets, and riversides of Bengal, cornering trade in the most valuable '*items-salt, saltpeter, opium, areca nut*, and *tobacco*, *Mir Qasim* repeatedly complained about the arbitrary and tyrannical nature of such conduct and the financial loss it inflicted on his treasury.[146] He pointed out that native servants and brokers (*gumashtas*) went about misappropriating and abusing the papers and other insignia of the company while forcing themselves into trade in everyday goods such as oil, *fish*, straw, *bamboo*, *sugar, ghee*, rice, and *betel-nut,* acting like insolent landlords, disregarding the officers of customs and tolls at the markets and warehouses, and unleashing violence on local villagers and traders. *Warren Hastings,* writing to the governor in 1762, noted that almost every boat he saw on the Ganges, whether it belonged to the company or not, was flying English colors. He also rued the fact that in many parts of the Bengal countryside, traders masqueraded as agents of the English or paraded around in the uniform of company troops.

Mir Qasim eventually decided to abolish all duties on inland trade for native traders and merchants, putting them at par with the servants and middlemen of the company. He also sought to end his puppet regime, abandoning the old capital city of *Murshidabad* on the northern reaches of the Bhāgirathī and refortifying the city of *Munger* in Bihar farther west up the Gaṅgā and away from the reach of the company. He also began to strengthen his musketry and artillery. In the end, however, Mir Qasim's ambition of creating an independent state in eastern India eluded his grasp. The company had already decided to remove him from power after he had abolished the duties on trade. *Mir Qasim* tried to find last minute military alliance with the *Mughals* and the nawab of Lucknow. Awadh which

---

146 Vansittart, A narrative of the transactions in Bengal, 1760-1764 (ed) AC Banterjee and B.K.Ghosh, Calcutta (1766), 1976, pp. 148 - 149.

proved to be insufficient. At the battle of Buxar in 1764, the English East India Company crushed the combined military forces of *Mir Qasim* the Mughal emperor *Shah Alam II*, and *Shuja-ud-daulah,* the ruler of *Awadh Mir Qasim* became a fugitive, never to return to *Murshidabad.* The importance of the English victory at Buxar could not be gainsaid. Following the defeat of the *Dutch* in 1759 and the rout of the French in 1760, it gave the company an opportunity to snuff out the political ambitions of *Awadh* and to humiliate the *Mughal emperor, Shah Alam II* - significant steps in the elevation of the English *East India Company* as the undisputed political masters of *Bengal.* It presented the prospects of a new arena of empire to Britian that would eventually assuage the loss of the American colonies. In 1765, the company pressed its advantage with the Mughal emperor, who had taken temporary refuge in an English camp, holding him to the terms of the Treaty of *Allahabad*, which included the transfer of the office of revenue collection (Diwani) of its three great eastern provinces - Bengal, Bihar, and Orissa - to *Clive* and the East India Company. For the next few years the company, having reinstalled old Mir Jafar on the throne of Bengal, reaped the immense spoils of agrarian revenue without having to assume direct responsibility for the administration of Bengal.

A Delta Famished

The *East India Company's* acquisition of the *Diwani* would be later heralded by the English statesman *Edmund Burke* as a "great act of constitutional entrance of the Company into the body politic of India.[147] The passing of this mantle was recognized by all native powers, but the day-do-day collection of revenue in Bengal, *Bihar,* and *Orissa* remained in the hands of *Reza Khan* and *Shitah Rai,* while the nawab was placed under the watch of the British resident stationed at *Murshidabad. Mir Jafar* died in 1765, and his reenage son, *Najm-ud-daulah*, was installed on his father's weat in 1765. *Mir Jafar* had squandered most of his fortune, and his son ruled for

147 Forrest George, The life of Lord Clive, vol. II, London, 1418.

only a year, dying in a state of near penury from a severe bout of fever. He had entrusted the entire burden of revenue collection to *Reza Khan*, who proved to be both ruthlessly efficient and corrupt at the same time.[148] As the new regime sought to ratchet up the collection of land revenue, eastern India was lurching toward a severe drought. Revenue officers began to detect widespread crop failure in 1768, and a sharp spike in the price of staples followed. To add to the miseries of the peasants, the monsoon rains stopped prematurely in September 1769. Governor *John Verelst;* his deputy, *Henry Cartier;* and the members of the council, however, did not heed these early warning signs. Taxes were being collected without let from the peasantry as late as January 1770, when rice was scarce but barley and wheat seemed plenty along the banks of the River Gaṅgā. Despite the rising clamor of food shortages, a further one-tenth rise on the assessment had been sanctioned for the coming year.

William Hunter, in his vivid account of the *Bengal famine* in the Annals of Rural Bengal, suggests that the scarcity of 1769-1770 appeared without warning, and the company was caught woefully unprepared to address the widespread and abject starvation of its new subjects. One third of the population was rumored to have pereished in the district of *Purnia* alone. The native officers who knew what was happening did not inform the council in time to prepare for relief. The *Bengali peasant*, writes Hunter, "bears existence with a composure that neither accident nor chance can ruffle." The complaints of victims, Hunter seems to suggest, did not reach the ears of the officials, because the starving masses accepted their late with silent forbearance.[149] There is not enough evidence to support or discredit this impression of multitudes starving and dying without a whimper, but the devastation wrought by the famine was

148 Khan, Abdul Majed, The Transition of Bengal 1756 - 1775, A study of Sayyed Muhammad Reza Khan, Cambridge, 2008, p. 100.

149 Hunter, W.W., Annals of Rural Bengal, vol. I, London, 1871, pp. 21-22.

quick and massive, with millions perishing within the space of a few months. To quote from Hunter's grisly account.

The husbandmen sold their cattle; they sold their implements of agriculture they devoured their seed grain, they sold their sons and daughters, till at length no buyer of children could be found; they are the leaves of trees and grass of the field.[150]

Exhausted from burials and cremations, people began to throw then dead into the Gaṅgā. The English resident stationed at the nawab's seat of power in *Murshidabad* reported that the living were feeding on the dead along with vultures, dogs, and *jackals*. Pestilence followed hunger. The smallpox epidemic that broke out across Bengal did not spare the life of *Nawab Saif-ud-daulah. Ghulam Husain Khan*, in his contemporary account, writes that entire villages and towns "suddenly disappeared from the face of the earth.[151] In 1772, at the end of the famine, Warren Hastings reported to the court of directors that close to one third of the population of greater *Bengal* had disappeared over the course of two to three years.

Hunter describes the famine of 1769-1770 as the most significant event in the *Gangetic delta*, one that shaped the course of the history of Bengal over the next forty years. *Edmund Burke,* in one of his lengthy speeches during the trial of *Warren Hastings,* described the Bengal famine as the singular episode that "*dishonored and disgraced*" the government of the *East India Company* in Bengal in the eyes of both England and Europe at large.[152] The French belletrist *Abbe Raynal* in his widely read Histoire philosophique des deux Indes pointed the finger directly at the policies and conduct of the company government for this "appalling famine in this the most fertile of lands"; they saw the warning signs of scarcity and

---

150 Ibid., p. 26.

151 Khan Tabtabai, Ghulam Hussain, Seir Mutaqherin or Review of Modern Times, Vol. III, Calcutta, R. Cambay, 1902, p. 26.

152 Burke, Edmund, The Works of Right Honourable E Burke. Vol. VII, London, 1889, p. 254.

still deliberately stowed away a large portion of the grain harvest for their own consumption and that of their native Indian soldiers. Notwithstanding the flurry of recriminations, company officials understood that the entire organization of land revenue had become corrupt and moribund. Young English supervisors of revenue such as Gerard *Gustavus Ducarel* appointd to the district of *Purnia* or *Boughton Rous* in Rajshahi, both in their early twenties, pleaded that it was nearly impossible for them to penetrate the labyrinth of arcane practices of assessment and collection of land revenue left over from Mughal times and the obtuse forms of Persian account keeping.[153] Whille some attributed the failure of custodianship to the inexperience and youth of the English officials, others blamed the suffering of the poor on the rapacity of native moneylenders, middlemen, and dealers of grain (*paikars and dalalws*). Ghulam Husain indicts the conduct of *Reza Khan* himself, who was found guilty of stopping merchant boats for extra levies and of running corrupt monopolies in rice and other necessities of life for illicit profits that "increased the calamities of the poor during the height of the famine.[154]

Richard Becher, the English resident at *Murshidabad*, observed at the onset of the famine in 1769 that the *East India Company's* accession to the management of land revenue had significantly worsened the living conditions of the common people.[155] It was, according to *Becher*, the very nature of the company's investments, its export of currency, and most of all, its connivance at the pitiless exactions of native functionaries that had intensified the crisis. Colonial historians examining the origins of the famine in the breakdown of the prevailing system of land tenure concluded that the taxation of Mughal Bengal had been a top-down affair, with too

---

153 Guha, Ranjit, A Rule of Poverty for Bengal, An essay on the idea of Permanent Settlement, Durkhans (1963), 1966, pp. 47-49.

154 Khan Transition in Bengal, pp. 216-19.

155 Extract of a letter from Mr. Bechar H Prsident dt. May 24, 1769 reports from Committee of House of Common, London, 1803, p. 931.

much leeway given to individual officials (*amils*), *zamindars*, and revenue farmers, who often imposed additional cesses (abwabs) for personal gain.[156] The famine, paradoxically, destroyed the old land revenue order of the lower *Gaṅgā valley* and gave the company a free rein to overhaul the entire structure of land tenure and taxation.

Famine and pestilence wreaked havoc along the agrarian heartland of the lower Gaṅgā valley through the year 1772. There had been a widespread desertion of villages and pastures, with multitudes of starving and destitute people flocking to *Murshidabad* and Calcutta for survival and accepting abject forms of servitude, including chattel slavery and the meanest forms of wage labor. Large tracts of formerly cultivated land had been turned to waste, leading to a crisis in the collection of taxes. In many districts British officials remained in the dark about the extent of arrears and acreage that could be reclaimed from waste. *Edmund Burke* inveighed in Parliament that corrupt officials, both English and native had profited handsomely from the Bengal famine, aggravating the distress of the famished the image of the company government across Britian and the rest of Europe. The dishonesty and bribery of the East India Company servants according to *Burke* was the original sin and "ruinous distemper" of British affairs in India. The calamity, historian and statesman. *Thomas Macaulay* later concluded utterly ruined Bengal, the richest province of the Mughal Empire - a veritable garden of Eden. No part of India possessed such natural advantages, both for agriculture and for commerce. He wrote; Bengal was blessed by the Ganges which, "rushing through a hundred channels to the sea, has formed a vast plain of rich mould . . . that rivals the verdure of an English April," and where rice, spices, sugar, and oils could grow with little effort. Nonetheless, in an unexpected way, the famine had given the company a second opportunity to reclaim the fields of plenty and overhaul the old fiscal - military regime.

---

156 Rambotham R. B., Studies in the Land Revenue History of Bengal, 1769-1787, London, 1926, p. 16.

The passage of the *Regulating Act of 1773*, which was a formal declaration of the company's intent to assume direct governance of its Indian territories, confirmed *Warren Hastings* as the new governor-general of India, he took over the charge of revenue collection from the hands of Indian intermediaries. In the previous year the office of the *naib diwan*, held by *Reza Khan* and *Shitab Rai,* had been discontinued, and the entire revenue apparatus (khalsa) transferred from *Murshidabad* to Calcutta.[157] The act, promising greater vigilance of Parliament over Indian affairs, fordable all gifts and presents from native subordinates, intent on rooting out the corruption rife among all ranks of company servants in India, especially Bengal. The famine of 1769-1770, disruption in trade and manufacturing following the conflict with the nawabs, and the chaotic disorganization in the collection of land revenue compelled the company to assume a much more direct and responsible administration.[158]

As the famine receded and the everyday economy of the Bengal country side came back to life, the company found its investments on very insecure footing. There was an urgent need to resettle parts of the famine - stricken country where millions of peasants had either perished or been uprooted from their fields. The future of British territorial possessions now hinged on a quick restoration of the agrarian economy of Bengal. Governor-General *Hastings* pushed through an extensive inquiry into the fallen state of land revenue collection, attempting to repair and secure the tenure of primary products whose welfare he thought ought to be the immediate care" of the British governmentin India - who needed to be protected

157 Misra, B.B., The Central Administration of the East India company 1773-1784, Bombay, 1959, pp. 114-115.

158 Sen Sudipta, Liberal Government and Illiberat Trade, The political Economy of Responsible Government in Early British India in Kathbu Wilson, (ed) The New Imperial History Culture Identified and Modernity 1660-1828 Cambridge, 2004, pp. 143-144.

against the ruthless exactions of despotic and rapacious landlords.[159] The reports submitted by the *Amini Commission* (1776-1778) on the condition of agricultural production in the eastern provinces pointed out that neither the appointment of English collectors nor the delegation of native officers overseen by the provincial councils had been able to stem the decline in land revenue. For years, instead of taxes, these officers had reported returns of deficit, along with details of defaulting *zamindars*, absconding farmers, and fleeing agricultural labourers. The Committee of Circuit in its reports on the revenue and commerce of Bengal stated that one of the major impediments to the free movement of "goods and necessaries of life passing by water through the interior of the country" was the petty *tyranny* of the myriad rural zamindars and farmers of revenue whose estates lay along the Gaṅgā and its various tributaries. They collected a plethora of dues and tolls on boats and caravans as part of their traditional claims over the passage of mercantile goods, listed under the head of sa'ir in Mughal accounts as separate from land revenue (*malguzari*).[160] Along key bends of the river and points along the overland trading routes, merchants, pilgrims, and travelers were accustomed to paying a repeated number of small duties - most commonly known as *rahadari* (highway tolls) and zakat (contributions) in exchange for safety of their goods and persons.

The scarcity of grain and its poor distribution had made it clear to officials of the company that the Gaṅgā and the vast network of waterways was essentially the pulse of life in the lower provinces of the valley. During the height of famine, *Shitab Rai* had been able to relieve the starving population of the city of Patna and its environs, a measure that saved thousands of lives.[161] A similar measure in *Murshidabad* did not succeed because desperate fights broke out

159 Firminger, Walter K. (ed) The Fifty Report from the Select Committee of the Housing Common of the affairs of the East India Company, Calcutta, PCCCXI.

160 Sen, Sudipta-, Liberal Government and Illiberal Trade, p. 148.

161 Hussain Seir Mutaqherin, pp. 55-56.

over boats transporting foodgrains, a armed militias of the elite at the various *ghats* wrested provisions away from the hands of the needy. Pursuant to the end of the Bengal famine, a new set of rules was passed to ease the passage of trade and commerce along the main waterways. District collectors were directed to stop all levies and tolls along the ghats of the Gaṅgā and its branches on boats plying between markets stretching from *Banaras* in the west of *Dhaka* in the east. These rules overturned the ancient and time-honoured rights of landlords and chieftains to claim a share from the profits of merchandise passing through their territorial jurisdictions. These prtty and customary duties were replaced by a string of custom houses set up by the company, with major establishments in Calcutta, *Huglī Murshidabad, Dhaka, Patna Manji,* and *Banaras* to monitor and tax all internal trade as the exclusive prerogative to the company state.[162]

This was not an easy task. For many years to follow, the outlawing of such privileges led to repeated conflict between company forces and local landlords along the banks and bends of the Gaṅgā. Over time, however, the custom houses of the company, supported by police outposts, were able to exert greatere authority over the passage of trade along the river, inspecting and stamping every boatload of goods alter payment of dues. After 1781, when *Hastings*, having extracted large sums of money in heu of troops from the raja of Banaras, Chait Singh, finally had him deposed, similar regulations of police and customs were extended along the course of the *Gaṅgā* at *Mirzapur, Banaras, Jaunpur*, and *Ghazipur*. Here, as in the Bengal delta such measures were obstructed by *zamindaqrs*, chieftains, and merchants who stood to lose the most in terms of power and profit, leading to widespread incidents of defiance including armed confrontations. *G.H. Barlow* who was sent by Governor-Genereal Lord Cornwallis to inquire into the state of manufactures and commerce in *Banaras* in 1787 and to report back to the court of directors about prospects of investment in that

162 Sen Sudipta, Empire of Free Trade, p. 98.

province, found that there were still myriad restrictions placed on the free movement of commodities due to the residuum of petty dues and exactions levied on trade. Once these impediments were removed, he wrote in one of his reports. "The navigation of the Ganges from the sea to its source would be freed from all obstructions, and the manufactures from Bengal and the exports from Europe would be transported to the heart of *Hindustan* at a trivial expense.[163] Toward the end of the eighteenth century, along the 400-mile stretch of the Gaṅgā plains between the cities of *Calcutta* and *Banaras*, the company government enacted and pushed through a series of economic reforms to put an end to the ancient and hereditary claims of local regimes on the passage on goods and market exchange.

The overhaul of the entire system of land revenue collection in Bengal, *Bihar* and Orissa has been the subject of extensive historical research, especially changes that took place in the 1790s during the tenure of *Lord Cornwallis,* who initiated a new regime of collection, validating by law the estates of the major *zamindars* of the Bengal presidency who were seen as amendable instruments in the creation of a colonial agrarian order.[164] This compelling vision of a new and improved landed society based on secure agricultural tenures and a propertied class of *rural landlords*, as historian *Ranajit Guha* argued in his definitive study on the subject, emerged from two decades of contentious debate among framers of the company's land - revenue polices.[165] With the passage of the *Permanent Settlement* in 1793, *Cornwallis* sought to reinstitute the *zamindars* of Bengal by stripping them of their old *quasi-feudal* privileges and inculcating the values of thrift, progress, 1 and capitalism as exemplified by the rural gentry of England.[166] A parallel set of reforms was passed

163 Barlow's Report on the Trade and Coinage of Banaras, Cited in Sen, Empire of free trade, p. 103.

164 Sinha, N.K. Economic History of Bengal from Plassey to Permanent settlement in Bengal, vol. 2, Calcutta, 1962.

165 Guha, Ranjit Rule of Property, 1996, pp. 104-197.

166 Ibid., p. 141.

during the same period integrating the various species of internal revenue, which included the resumption of rights over the various internal marketplaces - weekly hats, residential ganjs and qasbas, and markets for bulk produce such as *katras*, *mandis* and golas - aimed at rescuing market exchange from what company policy makers saw as the predatory and corrupt influence of native landed elements and religious institutions. Market duties were this taken away from the traditional class of landlords and made a part of company government's taxation; only those who could provide documents from the *Mughal era* supporting their claims were compensated with small deductions in land revenue. Thousands of markets set up between 1765 and 1790 were declared unauthorized, and their levies resumed.[167]

Between 1790 and 1815, revenue collectors of the company took on the exhaustive and painstaking task of securing control of marketplaces, pilgrimages, and fairs along the roads and waterways following the course of the Gaṅgā from Mirzapur and *Banaras* in the west to Calcutta and *Sagar Island* in theeast. How effective these proved to be in the long run is subject to debate, and some historians of the period, notably *C.A. Bayly*, have argued that the company, despite its unquestioned political and military mastery, was still financially *hamstrung* and beleaguered, heavily dependent on native intermediatries and financiers, its dictates compromised by the direct and indirect resistance from the various ranks of indigenous society. There is little doubt, however, that the Gaṅgā valley came under the direct purview of the company government. Captain *James Rennell's* military sketch surveys conducted over a period of seven demanding years, during which he nearly lost his life in an encounter with Sanyasi rebels, led to the comprehensive Bengal Atlas of 1781. *Rennell* wanted to plot the precise route of the Gaṅgā from the Himalayan foothills to the Bhāgirathī delta, improving upon the work of Jesuit Father Tieffenthaler, who had visited *Allahabad* and *Banaras* in 1765 and prepared a gargantuan 15-foot-

167 Sen Sudipta, Empire of free Trade, pp. 140-41.

long chart of the river. Rennell, a military engineer and the first surveyor general of British India, wanted more fastidious details. He was fascinated with how after winding for almost 800 miles through the cavernous and rocky slopes of the *Himalayas*, the Ganges "issues forth a deity to the superstitious yet gladdened, inhabitant of Hindoostan" taking theshape of a "smooth and navigable stream through delightful plains.[168] As a geographer, *Rennell* valued not only its alluvial bounty but its eminent navigability, especially as it served the interests of the company "in the capacity of a military way."[169] Rennell's Atlas yielded a commanding prospect of the Gaṅgā and its surrounding territories. Its accompanying inventory of maps is testimony to the enormity of the task the undertook, attempting to track every meandere along the course of the river, the elevation of its banks, the frequency and size of its seasonal islands and sandbanks, the forces of its current, the length of its gulfs, the levels of its water during the driest and wettest months, the soil quality of its banks, the number and convenience of its fords, the areas of its surrounding jungles, the size of its creeks and channels, the extent of its monsoon floods, the state of its inland navigation, and the exact quantities of water it discharged every season. His memoir, furnished with a comprehensive atlas, contains a detailed table of routes and distances upriver from Calcutta intended as a guide for inland navigation, along with 510 "water routes," taking into account the accessibility of ferries and fords during months of drought and monsoon floods. Further surveys of the main stretches of the river were conducted by his assistants William Richards, Luis Felix de Gloss, and Henry Huygens. These charts, along with a compendious tabulation of cities, towns, and markets lying along the main routes between Calcutta, *Murshidabad*, *Patna* and *Decca* (Dhaka) in the Description of the Roads in *Bengal* and Bihar are proof of the visibility and ascendancy of the company across the

168 Rennell, Jamu, Memoir of Map of Hindoostan or the Mogul empire, London, 1793, pp. 336.

169 Ibid, p. 337.

great plains of northern India toward the end of the eighteenth century. During the course of thenext century these passages would be further subdued and secured under the aegis of the Geographical Survey of India and the East Indian Railway Company, which laid down rails to connect to Delhi through Rajmahal and Mirzapur.

A New Landscape

During the eighteenth century, with the unraveling of the Mughal administration, travel via the markets, towns, pilgrimages, quays, ferries, and roads along the Gaṅgā-visited repeatedly by traveling armies - had become increasingly perilous. *W.H. Sleeman's* widely read Report on the Depredations Committed by the Thug Gangs of 1839, at the end of the company's long and bloody Thugee campaign, provides abundant details of the various denominations of stranglers and looters operating on the pilgrim routes along the river between *Allahabad, Mirzapur,* and *Banaras*, and farther north at the sacred precincts of Haridwar, serving large masses of pilgrims and traders many of their victims carriers of holy Gaṅgā water.[170]

Before law and order was reasserted by the *East India Company,* pilgrimages along the river were claimed by rival powers such as the Sikhs and the Marathas. Captain Thomas Hardwicke, who stopped at the fair of Haridwar on his journey to *Srinagar*, *Kashmir*, witnessed the clout of the Hindu ascetic and militant Gosains, wielding their swords to maintain a vigilant order at the bathing steps, collecting duties, imposing sanctions, and administering lashes to offenders. When fourteen thousand Sikh horsemen arrived nearby for ablutions, and *Sikh Udāsī* ascetics were sent to mark a spot by the rivedr with their flat, the Gosains attacked them and stripped them of money and belongings. Hardwicke saw the Sikhs dispatching an agent to recover damages and negotiate for a portion of the riverbank for their rituals. The dispute, however, had not been fully resolved, and the Sikhs ultimately exacted their vengeance on the Gosains. The

---

170 Sluman, W.H. Report on the Depredations Committed by the Thuq Gaṇgs of upper and Central India, Calcutta, 1840, p. 113.

bloody carnage that followed not only wrecked the pilgrimage but left five hundred Hindu ascetics and fifty Sikhs dead.

The scene described reveals the continuing power and prestige invested in the patronage of fairs and pilgrimages along the Gaṅgā. In Banaras, for example, where the great Rajput noblemen once underwrote the upkeep of the *ghats* and temples of *Banaras* during the reigns of Mughal emperors *Akbar* and *Shah Jahan,* the Marathas now asserted their preeminence during the greater part of the eighteenth century, striking an alliance with the nawab of *Awadh* and lavishly endowing the riverfront of the city that had once sheltered their leader *Shivaji* with many of its lasting structures. As the eminent historian of Indian antiquity *A.S. Altekar* aptly remarked, modern day Banaras was "largelya creation of the Marathas."[171] *Peshva Bajirao I* (1720-1740) endowed the *Maṇikarṇikā* and *Dashāshwamedh* ghats, and Queen Ahilyabai of Indore built the present Vishwanath temple (1775-1776). The city flourished under the patronage of the rajas of *Banaras, Balwant Singh* and *Chait Singh*, until the kingdom was annexed in 1782 by Warren Hastings for the *East India Company*. The patronage of Indian potentates continued even during the early period of company rule. *Baijabai*, the widow of *Daulat Rao Scindia* of Gwalior, built the pavilion around the holy well of *Gyān Vāpī* in 1828, and *Maharaja Ranjit Singh* of Lahore donated the gold filature covering the spires and domes of the *Kashi Vishwanath* templs in 1839. In 1765, as signatory tot eh Treaty of *Allahabad* ending the battle of *Buxar*, the *East India Company* acquired the confluence and pilgrimage of *Prayag*, which had been under the Mughal imperial charter and enjoyed the lavish patronage of heads of the Rajput princely states, the *rana of Nepal*, and kings and chieftains of *Kathiawad* and *Kashmir*.[172] Thus a vast concourse of trade and pilgrimage now came under the power and protection of the company raj.

171 Altekar, A.S. Banarawal Sarnath, Past and Present, Varanasi, 1947, p. 24 (BHU).

172 Mukherjee R. K. Allahabad, pp. 663-664.

Through its many custom houses the company attempted to keep a reliable account of the annual traffic of boats and the thirty-housand-odd boaters plying their trade between the markets and ferries from *Dhaka* to *Banaras*. Having declared that the inhabitants of India must be allowed a free exercise of their religious practices, the company resumed and consolidated all major duties levied on pilgrims by Indian local rulers and petty landed elite, adding to both their coffer of taxes and their administrative burden, paying no need to missionaries and other critics who felt that a Christian government should not be in the business of collecting revenue from the mass of poor pilgrims or interfere with the working of idolatrous Hindu charitable endowments.[173] As these passages became secure for travel, prospects along the Gaṅgā began to attract the attention of missionaries and tourists from England and Europe, including romantic travelers and professional arists in search of novel vignettes of Indian antiquity inspired by contemporary ideas of the naturalistic sublime and the *picturesque*.[174]

Back in England, artistic tastes of the time were moving away from classical formalism to the more inadvertent pleasures of the *picturesque*, which was a new form of gentlemanly, artistic pursuit popularized by enthusiasts such as Uvedale Price and *William Gilpin* - and emotive depiction in his classic work on the subject, from the cultivation of "*feeling the eyes*." Just as they would in the English countryside, a traveler in search of the picturesque in India was expected to discern the aesthetically pleasing visual properties of the Indian rural and natural landscape in which the River Ganges was one of the most eagerly sought subject. From the late eighteenth century through the early *Victorian era*, amateurs and professionals armed with pen, pencil, sketchbook, and watercolors labored tirelessly on the idylls and prospects of the river. Their prints brought

173 Cassels, Nancy G. Religion and Pilgrim Tax under the Company Raj, New Delhi, 1988, pp. 50-59.

174 Mitter, Partha much Maliqned Monster, A History of European Reaction to Indian Art, Chicago, 1992, p. 106.

alive exotic imprrial locales for viewers at home, contributing to a distinctly Gangetic view of England's northern Indian possessions. *William Hodges*, a draftsman from the South Pacific expedition, led by example, traveling up and down the river between 1780 and 1783, depicting ruins against quiet and contemplative backdrops of nature. *Hodges's* landscapes allude to timeless arcadia where human subjects are diminished to enhance expansive and majestic views of the Gaṅgā. His travelogues are littered with description of the river following through the rocks of *Kahalgaon* (Cologong) in Bhagalpur or descending thorough the passes of the Rajmahal Hills, "meandering and glittering through an immense plain, highly cultivated, as far as the extent of the horizon, where the eye is almost at a loss to discriminate the termination of sky and land."[175] Sailing from *Munger* to Calcutta, Hodges describes how the "inexpressible grandeur" of the Ganges filled his imagination, with its perennial fleet of boats, its crumbling ancient temples with their flights of steps leading to the water, along with its woods, forests, and hills reminiscent of the verdant parks of Old England.[176]

From 1786 to 1794, *Thomas Daniell* and his nephew William, following in the footsteps of Hodges, scoured the breadth of the river from the foothills of the *Himalayās* to Calcutta, using the camera obscura to great effect for the accuracy of scale and perspective. Their aquatints and engravings resulted in lavish and costly publications such as the series Oriental Scenery, released in six parts between 1795 and 1808, and a *Picturesque* Voyage to India, published in 1810.[177] Along with natural landscapes, the *Daniells* also had a keen eye for ruins of ancient buildings. They seized the opportunities presented by the military explois of the company to travel to the interior parts of India and indulge in what they saw as the "guiltless

175 Hodges, William, Travels in India, During the year 1780-1783, London, 1793, p. 24.

176 Ibid, pp. 25-26.

177 Archer, Mildred & Archer W.G., Indian Painting for the British 1770-1880, London, 1955, p. 12.

spoliations" of artists capturing the beautiful and the picturesque aspects of India and taking them back to Europe as trophies.[178] The Gaṅgā was often at the center of such landscape, not just in albums but also in travelogues and romances, especially in popular accounts written by women such as Fanny Parks, Maria Graham, and *Emma Roberts*. Roberts in particular wrote evocatively about native life unfolding by the banks of the river. She found the old city of Patna particularly appealing, with its tall riverefront havelis, its giant fig trees, and the remains of its "*Gothic*" gateway in dark red stone redolent of feudal Europe. The river here, brimming to its banks, became a mirror for the turrets, spires, and domes of the temples and mosques, making an "exceedingly imposing" coup d'oeil.[179] And there was also the timeless Banaras, the spirit of which she thought could not be adequately conveyed in writing. Only paintings - as the Daniells had shown in their aquatints and engravings - could convey its unique blend of the beautiful and the grotesque. The confused mass of the structures of Banaras that made up the "stupendous wall" spreading along the bank of the Gaṅgā captured for Roberts and element of *Gothic* wondr in the alchemy of nature and art in India.[180] Seen through the romantic tint of antiquarianism, such riparian vistas offered succeeding generations of *Britons* who visited, worked, and died in India a glimpse of something akin to an imperial sublime, with the Ganges and the land through which it flowed viewed as a tribute to a timeless India.[181] A popular traveler's guide in its rapt musings on the panorama of *palaces*, temples, mosques, pinnacles,

178 Daniell Thomas & Daniell William. A picturesque Voyage to India, London, 1810, p. ii.

179 Roberts Emma, Scenes and Characterstics of Hindostan with Sketches of Anglo Indian Society, London, 1835, p. 171.

180 Ibid, pp. 237-39.

181 Almedia, Hornione De & George H. Gilpin, Indian renaissance, British Romantiz Art and the prospect of India, Burlingtno, 2005.

minarets, shrines, and canopies declared that *Banaras* was "without question the most picturesque city in India."[182]

The *mutiny* and upheavals of 1857, which saw some of the bloodiest episodes of *carnage* in cities and villages along the length of the upper course of the Gaṅgā, including the much-reviled Cawnpore Massacre in which a mob attacked British women and children, could not in the end dispel this long-term view of the river. It is fascinating to see how the first photographs of Banaras, taken by Dr. *John Murray,* a British surgeon, shortly after the uprisings of 1857, ried to recapture this very ambience of contemplative serenity.[183]

During the first half of the nineteenth century, India under British rule had become a testing ground for some of the most pioneering advances made during the Industrial Revolution. With the advent of steam, the company government turned its attention to the greater *Gaṅgā* valley and the *Gaṅgā - Yamunā Doab* to extend irrigation, navigation, and investment capital by taking over the remnants of *Mughal* - era aqueducts, causeways, reservoirs, and bunds, and reenginerring an entire system of canals. They took over, for example, *Muhammad Abu Khan's* canal from the *Gaṅgā* northand northwest of the city of Meerut, which ran only for twelve and a half miles and was not more than fifteen feet wide, and also the old *Doab,* or *Eastern Jumna*, Canal near Meerut.[184] Such old waterways were seen as having little benefit to poor cultivators whose fields often were placed at a higher elevation. A reliable system of canals was a key to the irrigation required for lucrative crops produced in bulk such as sugarcane and rice. A number of proposals had already appeared on the desk of Governor-General *William Bentinck,* who was contending with a spate of violent monsoon floods, as Sir *Proby T. Cautley*, engineer and early architect of the Ganges Canal project,

182 Caine, W.S. Picturesque India - A hand book for European Travellers, London, 1891, p. 301.

183 Journal of the photo graphic society of Bangal, No. 3, 1867, p. 65.

184 Cautley, Proby T., Report on the Ganges Canal works, London, 1860, p. 6.

took up the post of supervisor of canals in Rohikhand and Delhi during 1837-1838, a devastating famine raged across the Central Provinces and the lower districts of the *Doab*, and the company government became increasingly wary of the rising cost of famine relief for its starving subjects.

Famine was a visible object, but he prospect of capital and investment in a regenerated valley struck the industrial ambition of the company-state, and soon the work of excavation started right next to one of the pilgrim spots, *Har-ki-Pauri* ("steps of Śiva"), near the holy city of Haridwar in the Himalayan foothills, Colonial engineers aided by an army of cheap native laborers dug through the centuries old alluvium of the floodplain (*khaddar*), charting a course from Kankhal to Kanpur, 325 miles downstream. They set up gauges to measure the discharge of the Gaṅgā at Hardwar *Garhmukteshwar, Fatehgarh, Kanpur,* and *Allahabad.* The object of the great Ganges Canal was to connect with the main river jetties of *Allahabad* opening up the entire waterway to steamer traffic. The *East India Company* saw canals as a means to ameliorate the impact of famines, which in India, much like in Ireland, were seen not so much a result of the scarcity of produce as the pitiable purchasing power of the masses living at the edge of subsistence. The Ganges Canal, instrumental in opening up the traffic of boats and steamers, was also seen as the conduit through which grains and foodstuffs from *Mirzapur, Banaras*, and *Calcutta* could be brought to the inland towns and *bazaars* of the greater *Doab*.[185]

A new faith was placed on the ability of machinery to harness the power and energy ofhe Gaṅgā. Canals would employ the starving poor in the undertaking and maintenance of masonry and earthworks.[186] The canal authorities also took over sacred sites, promising to ease the difficulties of millions of poor pilgrims beholden to their ritual ablutions, especially during spates and droughts, and to keep the bathing ghats of pilgrimages such as Haridwar safe for traffic. The

185 Smith, A Short Accounts of the Ganges Canal, p. 4.

186 Cautley Proby T., Report on Ganges Canal Work, p. 52.

canal was inaugurated on April 8, 1854 at Roorkee, the site of the first college dedicated to engineering in British India, which was now the new headquarters of the Ganges Canal project Charles *Eliot Norton,* writing for the North American Review, was greatly unpressed by the grand opening, writing that the word had now spread all across India and pilgrims were arriving from distant parts of the country to see for themselves that "the revered Gaṇges was about to leave her ancient and hallowed channel for one formed for her by the hand of strangers. Lieutenant-Governor *John Colvin*, in his inaugural toast lauding Colonel Cautley, declared that the British had finally left a "permanent mark on the soil of India to attest the power, the wealth, and the munificence of their nation. The British in India thus became the architects and custodians of one of the largest canal systems of the world, which with its main channel, branches, and terminal lines totaled 898 miles. Contemporary engineers like J.S. *Beresford* saw the canal as a "machine composed of may parts" that connected canals, distributaries, rural watercourses, and individual cultivators. [187]

Somewhere through the long apprenticeship of culture under the watchful eyes of a modern industrial empire, the Gaṅgā began to recede from its living, universal, empyrean presence and resemble - to borrow the words of India's first prime minister, *Jawaharlal Nehru* - "a symbol and memory of the past of India."[188]

---

187 Beresford, J.S. Memorandum dated August 1875 on the irrigation duty to water in Punjab irrigation Branch Papers, No. 10, 1906, p.2.

188 Nehru, J.L. quoted in Dorothy Norman, Nehru the first sixty years, Newyork, 1965, p. 574.

CHAPTER 4

SUMMING UP

GAṄGĀ, HER ORIGIN

In the vast subcontinent of India, fed by hundreds of streams that irrigate her fertile soil, *Gaṅgā* is yet a name to conjure with. To Indians *Gaṅgā* is not just a river among the many others in the country. She is the heavenly stream brought to the earth by the persistent efforts of many princes of *Sagara's* family, generation after generation, till at last one of them succeeded in coaxing her to come down not only to earth, but to proceed further to the netherworld, to purify the ashes of his ancestors, so that they could be assured absolution from their sins if any, and transportation to heaven, the waves of the stream acting as the steps of a staircase leading to the highest goal. It is in this context that Gaṅgā is considered a soaring ladder to heaven for the sons of *Sagara*: *svarga sopāna paṅktim.*

Gaṅgā origin in Brahmā's waterpot

Gaṅgā is the holy water in the kamandalu or the water vessel of *Brahmā*, the purest concept of knowledge of ritual and philosophic thought. The book in *Brahmā's* hand is a symbol of his vast philosophical knowledge, the highest para *vidyā*. The sruk or the sacrificial Iadle itself.[189]

Viṣṇupadi, Gaṅgā issues from the foot of Viṣṇu in the sky

When Vamana assumed the form of Trivikrama and encompassed the entire universe covering the total terrestrial area with one foot and the entire celestial sphere with his upraised left foot, *Brahmā* poured water on this in token of his worshipful attitude. The water that issued from the *kamanḍalu* of *Brahmā* cleansed the foot of Viṣṇu and flowed down to reach the *jaṭās* of Śiva ultimately. Gaṅgā is therefore Viṣṇupadi, the stream that emanated from Viṣṇu's foot. This is also a veiled expression of her origin in *Viṣṇupāda*, the sky. The term connotes both the foot of Viṣṇu and the celestial region. The sky itself is so called by virtue of its having been encompassed by the foot of *Viṣṇu* raised by *Trivikrama* as he covered the universe in his three strides.

On a door lintel from *Hampi*, an excellent example of late *Çālukyan* work, there is not only the *Trimūrti* shown in three panels that form its main decoration, but there is also intricate workmanship all around on the makara *toraṇa* design meandering from the gaping mouth of one makara to the other with tiny musical figures of ganas in all possible manner of tiny medallions formed by the undulating creeper design. At the top, there are exquisite miniature figures in groups composing and narrating scenes from the sacrifice of Bali, *Vāmana* begging for just a three foot space from Balik, the emperor of the demons, and his subsequent transformation into the universe encompassing Trivikrama. Over the foot raised towards the sky *Brahmā*, standing in respect, is shown pluring from his kamanḍalu the holy stream of *Gaṅgā*. This is a very graphic representation in an exquisite miniature sculpture panel of the celestial origin of the heavenly river. These miniature carvings on this long and interesting lintel, are often missed or unnoticed, but they are more significant than even the larger, because the glory of the *trinity* is narrated here,

189 Dr. Śivarama Murti, C. *Gaṅgā*, N. Delhi, 1976, p.1.

and particularly of Viṣṇu who completely covered the expanse of the universe thus justifying the name *Viṣṇu*, and from whose foot *Gaṅgā* herself issued and received the appellation, *Viṣṇupadi*.

Nupūragaṅgā

As *Brahmā* hurried to worship the foot of *Viṣṇu* raised skywards in his Trivikrama form, by offering water from his *kamanḍalu, Gaṅgā* originating from its, fell on the *nupūra* or the anklet, and from that dropped to the earth, almost of disappear in *Śiva's* locks, though probably untouched even by the jhatas. Thereform she descended as a tiny stream on Mount *Vṛṣabha* or *Alagarmalai*, and iks known as *Nupūragaṅgā*, or Gaṅgā proceeding from the anklet, who removes all sins. There is usually a belief tghat water when it drips from the hair is impure, but falling from the locks of Śiva which comprise one of the *pancamahābhūtas*, i.e. akasa or ether, *Śiva* being *Vyomakeśa*, it is entirely purifying and sanctifying. That is why there is a school of thought which is amused by even the thought of impiety voiced in the remark that those, avoiding a bath in the Ganges because it fell from *Śiva's* locks, are like those who do not bathe in theholy ocean as it is the abode of briny water:

na gahanṭe gaṅgām api harajaṭasāra it ye
na majjantyam bhodhau lavanarasavesantaka iti.

Venkatanatha's description of *Nupūragaṅgā* is indeed significant. On the summit of Mount *Vṛṣabha*, the eternal abode of *Viṣṇu*, here known as *Sundara* or the Beautiful One, a rare treasure to those devoted to him, is the sacred pool that issued from the anklet of the conqueror of *Bali*, i.e., *Trivikrama*, and appears to have reached here almost without touching the *jaṭās*, the locks of Śiva :

nityavasam vṛṣabham acalam sundarakhyasya visnoh
pratyasidan sapadi vinamad bhagadheyam natas syah
yasyotsange balivijayinas tasya manjiravantam
patho divyam pasupatijatasparsasunyam vibhati[190]

190 *Hamsasandeśa* I, 49.

A drop on Śiva's locks, but immaculate

Nīlakantha Diksita describes the mighty stream of *Gaṅgā*, the celestial river, as a drop of water at the top of one of the matted locks (*jaṭās*) of *Śiva*, and also as the most holy river for the entire universe, thereby stressing the glory of *Śiva* by whose touch even this river assumes special holiness: *yatkesagravilaynaṁ ambu jagatam tīrtham param pavanam* (*sivotkarsaṁanjari*). *Gaṅgā* is both purified by the touch of the Trinity itself, but what is more, she purifies everyone in the Trinity as well, which is more than can be said of any other stream.

Though she fills the ocean Gaṅgā is just a drop on Śiva's jaṭās

It would appear almost a wonder to know that the entire ocean, *Sagara* that dried up, was filled again completely by the surging waters of the Gaṅgā. The heavenly river could fill even the ocean! Thee is an interesting story of how in days of your, when the *Devas* and *Asuras* fought, the latter after harassing the former, hid themselves in the ocean, the waters of which were inaccessible to the former. At the request of the celestials themselves, *Agastya* proceeded towards the mighty ocean which he sipped in a trice for the welfare of the world. It was now easy for the *Devas* to destroy the Asuras who could no more hide themselves. After the *Asuras* were overcome, there was no more need for the ocean to be kept dry. In fact it was essential that the ocean be filled. The *Devas* now approached *Agastya* to release the waters sipped by him, but since he had already digested the waters of the ocean, the question of release could not arise; now the celestials had no other choice but to request *Brahmā* to help them refill the ocean. *Brahmā* reassured them that the ocean would be filled in time when *Bhagīratha*, by his penance, brought down the heavenly river *Gaṅgā* to the earth and took her towards the ocean to purify the ashes of his ancestors that lay on its bed. He foretold that the waters of the *Gaṅgā* would fill the ocean and this is indeed what happened. It is no wonder at all that the waters of a single river could fill the ocean. It is symbolic. All rivers are symbolized by *Gaṅgā* and she is herself the celestial stream. At any rate the glory of *Gaṅgā* in mythology makes it no great problem for her to fill the ocean, when the force of here descent from heaven required the mightiest of the mighty celestials, *Śiva* himself, to hold her on his locks, lest there should be a complete devastation of the world by the force of here fall :

> *mahata kalayogeṇa pṛakritim yasyate'ṛnavah*
> *jantimsca karaṇam kṛtva moharajo Bhagīraṭhah*
> *purayisyati toyaughais saundram nidhim aṁbhasam*[191]

The glory of Gaṅgā however, far exceeds that of the ocean as Nilkantha Diksita admits. The ocean itself was filled by the abundant waters of the stream of Gaṅgā; yet this *Gaṅgā* was herself just a drop on the locks of Śiva. That very ocean, which *Viṣṇu*, who had earned great renown by successive incarnations as *Varaha* and *Rāma*, and who, as the former had dived in to rescue the *Vedas*, and as the latter built a bridge across toreach Lanka, was filled and enlarged by the waters of the mighty stream of the *Gaṅgā*. Yet she in her turn was just a drop on the *jaṭās* of *śiva*:

> *setum yatra nibadhya yātrā vasudham uddhṛtya magnam pura*
> *vikhyato madhusudanas sa jaladhir yatsrotasa puritaḥ*
> *sa jahnavyāpi yajjatatanusikhalambambulesayita*
> *sa svāmi mama daivatam taditaro namnapi namnayate*[192]

Consequences of *Gaṅgā's* Pride

Gaṅgā, proud and overbearing

Even though she was born the charming daughter of the snowelad *Himālaya*, and though her sancitity was such that mere thinking of her was enough to cleasure all sins, *Gaṅgā* was still a *kuṭila* or crooked one. Nevertheless, legend has it that the gods carried her to *Satyaloka* a decide on offering here to *Śiva*. But poor *Brahmā*, even with his eight eyes, could not really gauge here and, noticing here

191 *Mahābhārata* 3, 106, 203

192 *Śivotakarsamanjarī* 6

wayward ways and overweaning pride, dismissed the suggestion of the celestials to unite her with Śiva. When *Gaṅgā*, though a child, opened her mouth to have her say in the matter, *Brahmā* cursed her into assuming watery shape, i.e., the form of a stream. Taking even this in her stride, the daughter of *Himālaya*, with here waves lofty like those of the ocean, played about in the vicinity of Brahmā himself, who, alarmed at the fury and rage of her streams and eddies, created vast embankments to control her pride. It is no wonder that *Gaṅgā's* temperament led her to argue with *Bhagīratha* asking him hown she cluld descend to the earth from heaven without devastating the universe itself. Even as she spoke to the supplicant *Bhagīratha*, whose attitude pleased here, she almost appeared to drown the entire universe by her words;

jagada sadyo jagaḍandamanḍalaṁ nimajjayantiva vacobhireraśa[193]

Even if I were to enter the netherworld, said she, the entire globe of the universe would go to pieces like a frail dry gourd. Your desire is to acquire the undying fame of bringing me to the earth and to the netherworld to purify and carry your ancestors heavenward. But you overlook the tremendous sin that you commit by creating a deluge everywhere through me, resulting in the extermination of all living beings. How difficult was it and how wonderful the manner in which *Brahmā* created this vast universe by the great effort of his yoga!

At one stroke, you desire to render this a mere memory in history, all by my descent on it. If through my deference to the word of *Brahmā*, who has allowed me to go with you, I put aside my natural compassion for all living beings and descend to the underworld, where would you be yourself to offer your respectful obsequies to your ancestors? My waves are not mere worlds, they are devastating in action. Show me someone to whom I can demonstrate the force of my current. It cannot *Agastya*, the sage who drank the ocean. Though I grieve to think of the devastation I would cause, I still rejoice that here I have a chance to give my waves full play, which

193 *Gaṅgāvataraṇa* 3, 1

I have long desired. If I suddenly enter *Amarāvatī*, the glorious city of the celestials, would Indra be able again to see the face of his beloved Sācī, whom he lovingly paints with perfumed sandal? Would it either be possible for the earth, which cannot be flooded by even the deep and placid waters of the great ocean, to bear the overwhelming force of my waters? *Bhagīratha* patiently listened to these proud words but again reitereated his desire to take her along with him, not in her *anthropomorphic* form, but as a stream, to purify and transport his ancestors to heaven. 'I am not asking you,' said he, 'to quench my thirst, there are many rivers for that. Nor even for water itself as such, there is rain for that. But I desire the water of your stream for purification. *Gaṅgā* finally agreed and promised to appear before him whenever he wanted. And now Brahmā again helped *Bhagīrathā* and assured him that Śiva was the only one who could receive the velocity of the descent of Gaṅgā's tremendous downpour. Indeed, it was Śiva the great God, a fraction of whose power destroyed the engire horde of celestials assembled at the sacrifice of *Dakṣa*, pleased with his devotion had blessed even *Mukunda* himself in the hoary past. By amile he destroyed the dreaded Tripuras. From him originated the four *Vedas* themselves and in front of him the mystic syllable Om could unravel his glory. He is beyond the universe, and all celestials hail him with one voice. He adorns one half of his body with his own vidya in the form of his beloved consort. He is the most auspicious, the immaculate, the omniscient, the eternal doer of good, the great lord, who has the entire universe at his feet. His abode is the crystal-capped silvery mountain, the humble citizens of whose capital are the Lord of wealth and prosperity himself and his *Yaksa* hosts, yet unrivalled in prosperity. He roams as a naked beggar with blades of grass, dhatturā and other flowers as decoration for his locks, rejecting only the alluringly sweet-smelling petals of *ketakī* as if it were a poisonous creeper. As *Bhagīrathā* prayed to *Śiva*, engaging himself in deep penance, which terrified even the celestials themselves, he occasionally heard at the time of twilight the sound of Śiva's drum, deep and rumbling, like the roar of thunder at the end of the deluge. There also appeared before him for a moment a galaxy of celestials stupefied by the imposing sight of the tandava of *Śiva*, the lord of *Candī*. Finally, Śiva himself graciously approached him and, to satisfy his desire, prepared himself to receive the heavenly stream. Gaṅgā came along with overweaning pride. 'I pity my father, the aged lord of the mountain, and my younger sister *Pārvatī* who has a loving heart, but if I proceed with my endeavour to come down, what is *Śiva* to me and what is this silvery mountain? I could envelope them both. Oh Brahmā! I have stayed long in your abode and it is on that account that I would like to oblige you. I shall now, as a punishment to *Śiva* who cut off one of your heads, drown him, deep in the netherworld, with my overwhelming waves enveloping the universe and swallowing up *Śiva*, reducing him to smitheing as it were, and mixing him up in my waters, so that pieces of his bones, like small bits of *śaṅkha* (*conches* and *shells*), may have to be fastidiously searched for by *Nandī*':

> *savalepanipatanmadurmibhissamplavaikakabalikrto haras*
> *sangatah payāsi sankhasuktibhīr nandīnd nānu*
> *gavesayisyate*[194]

Does *Śiva* take my turbulent water tobe somewhat like the *Kālakūta* poison that he once drank? Oh *Brahmā*! please even now desist from this request. I pity my sister who should not grieve for her lord. If, however, out of compassion for the universe you would ask lord. If, however, out of compassion fro ht euniverse you would who is so vain as to think he could hold my water. But *Śiva* just smkiled. And the monstrous stream came down with unparalleled velocity, destroying the entire celestial neighbourhood, even frightening *Saraswatī* in the mansion of her Lord's mouth, with a myriad celestials and heavenly sages all running helter skelter as the steeples of *Indra's Vaijayanta* palace crumbled and fell, With her

194 *Gaṅgāvataraṇa* 5, 7.

monstrous waves shining forth from the sbode of Brahmā himself up to the abode of *Himālaya*, and almost fondling her sister with them she entered the deep caverns in Śiva's locks, pushing out the skull of *Brahmā* himself, and thereby even the *Brahmahatyā* sin that Śiva had to encounter, and though, no doubt, purifying even *Śiva* as she could the entire universe, she just disappeared as a stream, and not a speck of her was seen anywhere else the moment she was caught and entrapped in *Śiva's* locks:

tajjatapatalakandarodarasvikrtas suranadimahormayaḥ
lesatopi kila nalalaksire satkriya iva krtaghnagocarah[195]

And, lo and behold! *Śiva's jaṭās* looked fresh but wet and gleaming, with the serpents undisturbed, the moon unruffled, and the crest adornment of fresh flowers unaffected; only their perfume was increased by the sweet-smelling blossoms of the celestial trees washed in abundance on to *Śiva's* locks by the heavenly stream :

aklistappannagam ajarjaritendurekham
avyastakasakitavastabakavatamsam
sambhor adrsyata siras
surasindhumuktadivyadrumaprasavasaurabhasarasandram[196]

Gaṅgā's overweaning pride is best seen in this vivid description of *Gaṅgāvataraṇa* by Nilakantha Diksita, where, not nulike Manmatha who boasted to *Indra* and the *Devas* that he could stir up and overcome even the great wielder of the bow, *Pināka*, *Gaṅgā* proclaimed how easily she could descend with tremendous force on *Śiva's* head and carry him down to the netherworld, pounding and reducing him to smithereens adding sarcastically that *Nandī* may have to search in vain for any trace of his bones. But her eventual fate reveals the excesses of here indiscretion. It is a vivid picture of Gaṅgā, immature, girlish, unacquainted with the superior power of *Śiva*, which has led to even great poets having a dig at here while describing lack of judgement. *Bhaṛtrhari* feels that those who are

195 Ibid 5, 9.
196 Ibid 5, 66.

devoid of discrimination would encounter a sad fall in a myriad directions, giving the vivid example of *Gaṅgā* who, falling from heaven on to the head of Śiva, descended there from on a mountain top, from the height of which she ran down to the earth, finally to reach the sea, where comming ling in that large mass of water, here own stream became insignificant and shed its identity, reducing here to on enviable state indeed :

siras sarvam svargat pasupatisirastah kṣitidharam
mahidhraduttungad avanim avanescapi jaladhiṁ
adho gaṅgā seyam padam upagata stokam athava
vivekabhrastanam bhavati vinipatas satamukhaḥ[197]

Jagannātha, however, has a wonderful way of explaining why Gaṅgā who arose from the lotus feet of *Viṣṇu*, and found a home in the golden locks of *Śiva*, should descend in a deep fall to reach the netherworld itself. It is not, as in Bhaṛtrhari, who chooses to use *Gaṅgā* as an example of lack of discrimination, that leads to a bad fall. 'O mother!' addresses Jagannātha, your origin is on the immaculate lotus - tinged toenail of the lord of the Lotus - princess, *Śrī*; your abode is in the palace composed of the locks of the opponent of Cupid: but all your activity beyond this is to liberate from sins and transport to heaven in immaculate form all those that are lost, having reached the lowest depths of degradation. O mother! is that fall of yours a fall at all, considering its purpose of self - sacrifice, which at once raises your personality to the greatest heights that even the celestials cannot hope to reach?

samutpattih padmaramanapadapadmanalanakhat nivasaḥ
kandarpapratibhata jaṭājutabhavance
athayam vyasango hatapatitanistaranavidhau
na kasmadutkarsas tava janani jagarti jagati[198]

---

197 *Bhaṛṭrharisubhāsita* 1, 10

198 *Gaṅgālaharī* 21.

And naturally he queries whether among the many rivers and streams running along the mountain slopes and adorning the b road plains there is any that has had the good fortune to mount up to and nestle in the locks of the Destroyer of the *Tripurās*, or any that has had the good fortune to wash the feed of the lord of *Śrī* with the waters of her stream. How can any of these then hope tot even approach in comparison the celestial river, even if poets would love to describe the rivers in hyperbole:

nagebhyo yantinam kathaya tatininam katamaya
purāṇam saṁhārtus suradhuni kapardodhiruruhe
kāya va sribhartuh padakamalam aksali salilais
tulaleso yasyam tava janani diyeta kavibhih (Gaṅgālaharī 22)

The story of *Gaṅgā's* descent pleases the *Manes* and *assures* them a place in heaven.

The happiest story narrated by the sage *Viśvāmitra* to the young boys *Rāma* and *Lakṣmana* as they listened with rapt attention, was of the descent of *Gaṅgā* to the earth, first on Śiva's *jaṭā*, and there from released, here flow into *Bindusāras*, whence she multiplied herself into seven streams, Hadini, *Pavani*, Nalini (eastward bound), Sucaksu, Sita, Sindhu (westward bound) and Alakananda following the course of *Bhagīrathā* to reach the ocean and the netherworld. This chapter in the *Rāmāyaṇa* is the one specially chosen for recitation even today to entertain those invited to dine on the *srāddha* day in any Hindu household. It is believed that listening to *Gaṅgāvataraṇa* from the *Rāmāyaṇa* purifies and assures the highest place in heaven even to the *Piṭrs* or the *Manes*. The ritual of reciting extracts from the *Purāṇas* and *Itihāsas* is fulfilled by the mere reading of the *Gaṅgāvatraṇa* chapter, even if more is not possible:

dhanyam yasasyam ayusyam putryam svargnam ativa ca
yas sravayati vipresu ksatriyesvitaresu ca
priyante pitaras tasya priyante daivatani ca[199]

---

199 *Rāmāyaṇa* 1, 44, 21-22.

Gaṅgāvataraṇa

Among the different earāṇas in *Bharata's Nāṭyaśāstra*, *Gaṅgāvataraṇa* is the last and most important. Gaṅgā's flowing onto the *jaṭās* of Śiva was such an event that the special manner in which she amended anthropomorphic form created a karaṇa representation, the artistic and suggestive. Normally in all forms of *Gaṅgādhara*,Gaṅgā in mermaid fashion is made to approach from above, not head first but in the normal way, letting herself down with hand clasped in adoration; but in *Gaṅgāvatarana karaṇa* she is shown descending head first with her hands and legs in a position suggesting diving and swimming; she even suggests the stream itself which is most fascinating, especially in the case of a river. It is only in Nepal that this *Gaṅgāvatarana* tradition is wonderfully preserved and associatedwith Śiva as *Gaṅgādhara*, iconographically a special form in this region. *Gaṅgā* descends onto Śiva's locks in exactly the same pose as the *karaṇa* of that name described by *Bharata* and illustrated in the sculptural panels with incised labels from the text on the *gopura* at *Chidambaram*. The sculptor has chosen the fluttering garment, *uttariya*, of *Gaṅgā* to add movement and tempo to the action of the stream, furiously descending from heaven onto the locks of *Śiva*.

In sculpture, *Gaṅgā* is shown as a devotee with her hands folded in *anjali*, descending onto the *jaṭās* of Śiva, all her earlier pride lost, with no hope of fulfilling her earlier plans of coming down with a tremendous force to drown and scatter *Śiva*, reduced to smithereens, far down in the netherworld from his high state on the *Himālayas*. She is now perfectly conscious of his superiority, and is almost a saraṇārthinī to the great *sāranya*, *Śiva*. He just points two fingers to one *jaṭā* from among the myriads of locks on his head, significantly suggesting that now, like a drop of water, she would remain on it. Most insignificant indeed is this drop, where a mighty stream that threatened to drown the universe is concerened. *Gaṇādharamūrti* in this aspect is signified by Nilakantha Diksita as humbling *Gaṅgā's* pride almost as a *saṁhāramūrti*, though he would not take away the life was the culprit stream. While he accepted here as one of his consorts next to *Pārvatī* herself, he reduced her supreme ego and thereby her pride. That is why Nilkantha Diksita puts on par, Madanantaka, the form of *Śiva* that punished *Madāna* who prided himself on being able to mortify the entire universe, *Tṛipūrāṅtaka* who burnt the brazen cities, and *Gaṅgādhara* conceived as *Gaṅgāsosanamūrti* rather than the mild and gracious receiver of the stream. However all this, he maintains, was done by Śiva only to admonish these three and with no malice or rancour, as he nevertheless gave a fresh leave of life to *Madāna* and admitted *Gaṅgā* to the high stgatus of his own consort;

> *gaṅgāmbhahpariśoṣaṇam smaramadocchedo jagadvaha*
> *ityadyam*
> *nigrahavaisasam kalyate kanthaduparyeva yāḍ.*[200]

GAṄGĀ AS ŚIVA'S CONSORT

Gaṅgā as Cāmaradhariṇi

In sculptures from Bangaladesh of *Śiva* dancing on the bull, there is a peculiar representation not of *Gaṅgā* and Yamunā flanking Śiva as described by *Kālidāsa* in the *Kumārasambhava* in the line murte ca gaṅgāyamune tadanim sacamare devam asevisatam, but of Gaṅgā on one side on her *Makara* and *Pārvatī* herself on her lion, gently saying the camara for their lord. It is here a peculiar but clear admission of the fact that *Śiva* also has two consorts like *Viṣṇu* or *Brahmā*, the former with *Śrī* and Sarasvatī in North Indian representation and *Śrī* and *Bhūdevī* in South Indian carvings, the latter with *Sarasvatī* and *Sāvitrī*, the last only very occasional in sculptural representations as from the door lintel from *Gaṅgārampur*, *Gaur*, now in the Indian Museum. A clear mention of Śiva with two consorts, Pārvatī and Gaṅgā, is found in a Cambodian inscription, and there is mention also of a sculpture of Śiva with both his consorts flanking him, made in gold by a Cambodian king. Like *Rājarājeśvarī*, the consort

200 Sīvotkarsamanjarī 45

of Śiva, attended by *Śrī* and Sarasvatī flanking her curis in hand, *sacamararamavanisavayadaksinasevita*, *Śiva* as *Naṭarāja* has, in his two consorts, not only two witnesses of his dance, but two *cāmaradhariṇīs*, *Gaṅgā*, exclusive of *Yamunā* in this case, and in the company of *Pārvatī* makes this all the more interesting.

Gaṅgā approaches Śiva as his bride

Gaṅgā, as she proceeds from one area to the other, gains experience. By the time she flows in all three areas, she is tremendously mature. She realizes that it is her great good fortune to be the consort of the Lord of the universe. It is this *Gaṅgā* who approaches *Śiva* as a shy, coy bride in a remarkable Gupta sculpture from *Rajouna*, in Bihar. She approaches *Śiva* on here vehicle, makara, not standing but very respectfully kneeling on the back of the crocodile, here hands demurely clasped in *Anjali*, exactly as a bride would timidly approach her newly wedded lord, but yet as a princess with the royal umbrella held over her head by a maid; and *Śiva* graciously holds out one of the locks of hair as the place of her abode. *Gaṅgā* is here clearly depicted as a *nayikā*, lovingly approaching her beloved one, and this is not merely *Gaṅgāvataraṇa* but *Gaṅgāpariṇaya* of *Śiva*. *Gaṅgā* is not shown here in mermaid form but in pure and complete *anthropomorphic* flgure as she is unually depicted on door jambs. There is no other representation of *Śiva* AS *Gaṅgādhara* receiving his bride graciously, except in this unique sculpture. *Śiva,* ever gracious towards his devotees, is equally gracious to the repentant *Gaṅgā* who comes to him with humility, and cannot refuse here protection where she seeks it.

Gaṅgā is a co-wife with Pārvatī

This leads on first to *Gaṅgā* as one of *Śiva's* two consorts along with Pārvatī. While there is distinct displeasure on the part of *Pārvatī* in all Indian representations of *Gaṅgādhara* where *Śiva* receives *Gaṅgā*, it is just the opposite in Cambodia. Here, she is a happy *co-wife* along with *Gaṅgā*. How they both come together in great affection and regard is clearly represented in the Mebon pillar inscription of *Rajendravarman* (A.D. 952), which states that, abandoning the company of other gods, and with devotion and reverence, this king sought with a longing the blue-throated *Śiva* in exactly the same manner as *Gaṅgā* and Bhavani:

> *vihaya sangam paradevatasu sraddha co bhaktis ca pare yadiye sṛikantham utkanthataya prapanne gaṅgābhavanyāviva devadevam.*

Another inscribed pillar of *Indravarman* from *Bakon*, not only narrates how a sculpture of *Śiva* as the lord of *Umā* and *Gaṅgā*, *Umāgaṅgāpatisvara*, was established but also how lovingly and with mutual faith *Gaṅgā* and *Umā* embrace Śiva from either side. *Indravarman* established the sculpture *Umāgaṅgāpatiśvara* in the attitude of his being embraced on the hip by the delicate hands of *Umā* and *Gaṅgā*. An excellent sculpture from Bakon, though mutilated, depicts Śiva flanked by *Umā* and *Gaṅgā* embracing him:

> *umāgaṅgābhūjalatasamslistajaghanasthalaṁ sa iśvaram sṭhāpitavan umāgaṅgāpatiśvaraṁ.*

Another long inscription at *Kapilapura* describes *Śiva* in the company of Bhavani and *Jāhnavī*, i.e., *Umā* and *Gaṅgā*, *bhavanījahnavīyuktam*. This follows the tradition in *Bengal* where *Umā* and *Gaṅgā* flank *Naṭeśvara Śiva*, even waving cauris for him, of which the finest example from *Sankarbandha* is to be found in the Dacca Museum.

The displeasure of Pārvatī who turns her face away from *Śiva* in vexation and anger at the prospect of a co-wife, Gaṅgā, is a favourite theme in art all over India. *Kālidāsa* hints at this when he describes how *Gaṅgā*, laughing through her foam almost tauntingly, and with a playfulness all her own at *Umā's* furrowed countenance, almost to further irritate her, caught the locks of *Śiva* with her hands, like waves, clutching at the crescent moon:

gaurivakṭrabhrūkutiracanam ya vihasyeva phenais
sambhoh kesagrahanam akarod indulagnormihasta[201]

The treatment of this subject starts very early, as in the *Gaṅgādhara* at *Elephanta* itself, Devī's face is tilted with her displeasure clearly indicated in her mein. It is all the more evident in still later sculptures as at *Gaṅgāikonḍācolapuraṁ* where the great emperor *Rajendra* took pride in bringing *Gaṇges* water to his new capital and gave great prominence to this form of Śiva as *Gaṅgādhara*. *Pārvatī* is so vexed at the prospect of being a *co-wife* that her face is turned away from even her most auspicious lord. *Śiva*, who, however, graciously appeases here with coaxing words and soft caressing of her chin and praise of her great beauty, unsurpassed by and impossible in any other.

This anunaya leads us to the other question of a satha or a rogue who appeases his jealous wife after delaying with another and disappointing the former. It is this aspect of the lover that is referred to in a *Nandī* verse of the *Mudrārākṣasa*, whee *Pārvatī* searchingly questions *Śiva* who hides *Gaṅgā* in his matted locks and evades her questions with clever replies. Who is this blessed one on your head? asks *Pārvatī*. It is Śaśikalā (the crescent moon), quickly answers *Śiva*. Significantly, again *Pārvatī* questions, Is that her name? and *Śiva* rebuts, It is no doubt the term for it; and how is it that thtough it is quite familiar you have forgotten it? *Pārvatī* has no other recourse but to speak out almost bluntly, I am asking of a woman and not the moon. But then, Śiva lovingly tries to wriggle out, Let *Vijaya* explain if you do not trust the moon. The duplicity of *Śiva* in this strain in trying to hid the heavenly stream from *Devī* is the poet's lovely creation of an imaginary conversation between them:

dhanya keyam sthita te ṣirasi śaśikala kim nu namaitad asya
namaivasyas tadetat paricitam api te vismrtam kasya hetoh
narimprcchaminendumkathayatuvijayanapramanamyadindur

201 *Meghadūta* i, 50.

devya nihnotum icchor iti surasaritam sathyam avyad vibhor vah.[202]

The same idea of the wife's jealousy at the prospect of a co-wife, and the rush of anger that the husband tries to appease is also clearly manifest in the opening verse of the *Tiruvalangadu* plates, where Śiva, the wearer of *Gaṅgā* on his locks, is this time unnecessarily suspected by *Pārvatī* who mistakes her own image reflected in the ruby on the hood of the serpent ornament and spurns him though he most lovingly is at her feet, desiring her close embrace:

svasti srikanthakanthabharanbhujagaranmudhni
manikayamadhye
drstvatmiyam salajja pratikrtim aparam anganam sankamana
aslesalolacittam krtacarananatiprarthanam vo bhavani
disyat pasyantyadhiram nijapatim anisam sersuam
ardhekṣanena[203]

Release of Gaṅgā in Gaṅgāvisarjanamūrti

Śiva's matted locks are a large cauldron, in which *Gaṅgā*, caught with all the fury of her mighty waves could only lash them from side to side, creating the effect of a dance of waters on the dancing *jaṭās* in the swirling movement of the supreme dancer *Naṭarāja*:

jatakatahasambhramabhramannilimpanirjhari
vilolavicivallari virajamanamurdhani

The swirling movement of *Śiva's* head in *tāṇḍava* releases *Gaṅgā* from the tips of the *jaṭā*, creating an impression of the heavenly river issuing from the dandapada of *Viṣṇu* in his incarnation as *Trivikrama*:

lilavadhutasirasosya
valajjatagranisyandisandrosaliloksitakotibhagat

---

202 *Mudrārāksasa* 1.1

203 South Indian Inscriptions 3, p. 383

uccandatandavarasasya vinirjagama mandakini madhuripor iva dandapadat[204]

The ocean is not only swollen by the waters of the *Gaṅgā* as described by *Venkatanātha* who fancies them not only pure and white like the moonlight flowing with the intent of increasing the ocean from the clear sky from the foot of *Viṣṇu*, but tinged on all sides and flowing in different directions, giving up its red colour by association with the sona river, having absorbed the dark waters of the *Yamunā*, the daughter of the sun:

visodhitat sāgaravvrddhihetor visvanmukhi Viṣṇupadat saranti tomomayim suryasutam nigirya jyotsnanadi sonam api vyamuncat[205]

Like the moon who gladdens the ocean by swelling her abundant waters, *Gaṅgā* also swells the ocean as the poets have often described. It is the same idea that occurs in *Mankha's* poem, where he describes the fall of *Gaṇges* water shaken during his dance, from the locks of the moon-crested *Śiva*, and the misting over of moon stones with the effect of the lunar rays that swell the ocean and magnify the volume of the heavenly stream:

sandhyatandarvivlasasamsaraccandrasekharasivassarijjalaih puryamana iva niradhir dadhe vrddhim indudrsadambubhid saha[206]

Could Yamunā also be a co-wife of Gaṅgā ?

Not satisfied with one disappointment for Pārvatī in the shape of *Gaṅgā* taken on the locks of *Śiva* as a petted and fondled and almost zealously guarded bride, *Ratnākara* describes the supposed presence of *Yamunā* also as an additional cause for vexation, but this time the quarrel is almost between the two streams themselves, *Pārvatī* not being part of the squabble. The poet feels that the ringe

---

204 Haravijaya 2, 49

205 Yadavabhyudaya 2, 70

206 Śrikanthạcarita 10, 23.

of blue on *Śiva's* throat is the embrace on the neck of the blue stream of *Yamunā*, in an attempt to assert her right to an equal place in the lord's affection like *Gaṅgā* herself, bringing in the jealousy of another *co-wife* to disturb the already ruffled domestic peace:

yasyanuragavasatas sphutakalakutacchayacchalena
krtakelika
cavamardam
irsyanubandhakalusam prasamiksya gaṅgām
alingito yamunayeva vibhati kanthah[207]

1. ADORNMENT OF ŚIVA

Gaṅgā turns a dancer

The *tanḍava* of Śiva is so contagious that edven the moon on his locks joins in. No wonder that with all her waves, *Gaṅgā* herself dances. In here dance *Gaṅgā* herself looks like a nati or a danseuse limitating the dance of *Śiva* himself with her upsurging waves, the waters of which destroy all sins and look like the hoods of the serpent, *Śeṣa*, bright in a flood of moonlight or like the tall peaks of the snowclad *Himālayas* moving in violent action, but especially resembling the arms of *Śiva* spread out and thrown up in the ecstasy of the tānḍava dance. This is how an inscription of *Vidyadhara Bhanjadeva* would have it:

sesaher iva ye phanah pravilasantyudbhasvarendutvisah
praleyacalasrngakotaya iva tvanganti yetyunnatah
nrttatopavighattita iva bhuja rajanti ye sambharas
te sarvghavighattinas surasarittoyormayah pantu vah.[208]

The poet *Trilocanacārya* accounts for the excellence of *Gaṅgā* as a great dancer by her close association with *Mahanta* and compares his own gush of poetry to the sweet sound of the anklets of a divine dancer, particularly to the flow of the heavenly river herself:

---

207 Haravijaya 1, 39

208 Epigraphia Indica IX, p. 275

mahanatajatacchatanatadamandamandakini
kalakvanitakankanavrajavikjrmbhivaggumbhanah
kavih kavikulodbhavo bhuvanabhavyadivyodayas
sivagamavisarado jayati saradavallabhāḥ[209]

Jagannatha Pandita imagines a very interesting picture of the dancing *Gaṅgā*. He fancies how her moving waves indicate the graceful movement of the myriad hands of a great goddess who has chosen a wonderful golden stage on the golden locks of dancing Śiva, who is himself celebrating his victory over the *Tripurās*, and the sound of the stream of *Gaṅgā*, deep and rumbling as it enters the caverns in *Śiva's jaṭās*, produces the noble note of the *damarū* to serve as the rhythmic echo of the dances drum, almost creating a new *taṅḍava* by the celestial stream in the wake of *Śiva's* more famous one :

pradosantarnrtyatpuramathanaliloddhrtajata-
tatabhogarenkhallaharibhujasamtanavidhutih
bilakridakrodajjala damarudamkarasubhagas
tirodhattam tapam tridasatatinitandavavidhih[210]

Elsewhere he very significantly fancies that Gaṅgā's dance, expressed through her waves suddenly shooting up and spurting, is not without reason. *Śiva*, passionately fond of the game of dice, which he usually plays with his beloved one, *Pārvatī*, stakes his precious objects like the snake, the hides of the lion and elephant, his own troops of impish *pramathas*, his necklace of *rudrāksa* beads, even his vehicle, the lofty *Nandī* bull and his charming crest jewel, the crescent moon, nearly exhausting all his resources. Having lost them all, but still unabated in his ardour for the game, he stakes himself and there arises a happy moment for the daughter of Himavan, Pārvatī, to softly smile significantly, and look with a twinkle in her eye at her *co-wife* perched on the golden locks of *Śiva*, almost as if to say 'Now I have yu in my hands, where at *Gaṅgā*

209 Ibid III. p. 63
210 *Gaṅgālaharī* 38

wakes up to averet the calamity by throwing her waves up high reminding *Śiva* of his greater, more fascinating pastime, tāndava, the dance of ecstasy, almost calling him to leae the game of dice and enjoy his *tanḍava* dance by commencing the movement of his limbs in response to themovement of *Gaṅgā's* waves :

> *dyute nagendrakrttipramathaganam anisreninandindumukhyam*
> *sarvasvam harayitva svam atha purabhidi dark panikartukame*
> *sakutam haimavatya mrdulahasitaya viksitayas tavamba*
> *vyalolollasivalgallaharinataghatitandavam nah punatu*[211]

Even as *Gaṅgā* echoes the dance movement of *Śiva* himself in his *angahāras*, *karaṇas* and the tossing of the head, the river flows out to form a backdrop for his dance :

> *viksiptabahunivahasya vihasya diksu*
> *tasyangaharakaranakrama-*
> *kampimurdhnah*
> *agratipatisalila surasindhur apa chindmsukojjvalatiraskarini-*
> *vilāsaṁ*[212]

Gaṅgā for *Śiva's aharya*

Gaṅgā serves in every way to enhance the beauty of *Śiva* particularly in his *aharya abhinaya*, as his choice of the heavenly river as an adornment for his *jaṭās* is only indicative of his great taste and discrimination. If *Mammata* feels that the beauty of the female breast is beest perceived when it is half hidden by a veil, the *jaṭā* of *Śiva* is of such great natural beauty that it is appreciated better when it has as a thin veil, the stream of the *Gaṅgā*. The heavenly river, with her mass of water fills the sky, shakes the sun and other planets by her velocity, derides the ocean with her wealth of waves and white as the moon acts as a graceful veil for the crest, fast bound by graceful tresses, of the moon-crested lord:

---

211 *Gaṅgālaharī* 38
212 *Haravijaya* 2, 27

vegoddhutaryamadigrahagaganatalam yasnuvana jalaughair
nyakkurvana samudran ksayavalitajalan urmimalasahasraih
deyad abhyarthitam vas sasadharadhavalasvardhuni candramauler
maulau litam vahanti sphutavikatajatabandhane cirikayah[213]

Gaṅgā, a flower garland or even a silken turban for Śiva

The immense power of *Śiva* whose dance shakes the world, is also suggested by vividly portraying the sudden transformation of the forceful stream of *Gaṅgā* into the speck of a flower on his *jaṭās* - *Gaṅgā*, whose force pulled the planets, the sun and the moon, tearing asunder the quarters, putting to shame the pride of the waters of the deluge in their monstrous surging waves - losing her individuality the moment she touched *Śiva's jaṭās,* where she immediately assumes the charming position of a flower for his matted hair :

vegakrstagraharavisasivyasnuvanam digantan
nyakkurvanam pralayapayasam urmibhangavalepam
muktakaram hara tava jatabaddhasamsparsi sadyo
jajne cudakusumasubhagam varik Bhāgirathīyam[214]

The lovely stream of *Gaṅgā* is fancied as resplendent as a garland of malati flowers on the head of Śiva making him look almost a dandy, a spngari:

devah payat sa vas sriman srngari girijapriyah
yasyu Gaṅgā jata jute malatimalikayate[215]

Bāṇa is undoubtedly the inspirer of this thought as he describes the white stream of *Gaṅgā* as a *mālatimālā*, a garland of malati flowers adorning *Śiva's* head :

andhakāmathanamaulimalatimalikam[216]

---

213 Epigraphia Indica II, p. 120
214 *Anamayastoṭram* 13
215 Epigraphia Indica XXXII, p. 137
216 *Harṣacarita* I, p. 7

Bāṇa's fancy does not stop here. He even imagines that *Gaṅgā* settled on Śiva's head is like a silken turban:

amsukosnisapattikam iva sumerunrpasya (Harsacarita I, p. 8)

Halayudha feels exactly like *Bāṇa* with the celestial stream trailing on *Śiva's* like a garland of *malati* flowers:

maulau lagna tridasatatini malatimalikeva[217]

Gaṅgā, a royal attribute, camara or umbrella

Gaṅgā is also the camara, insignia of royalty for *Śiva* whose golden locks are as a crown with the hoods of the serpent acting as an umbrella on top. The moon rather is *Dvijarāja*, a king, and he sits on the golden throne of *Śiva's jaṭās* with the waves of the *cauri* provided through the spray of the *Gaṅgā*, the white snake garland with uplifted hoods serving as an umbrella over him :

yatsimhasanam iśvarasya kanakaprayam jaṭāmanḍalaṁ
gaṅgāsikaramanjariparikarair yacca maraprakriya
svetotphullaphanancalas sivasirassandanadamoragas
chattram yasya jayatyasavacaramo raja suddhadidhitih[218]

The *Gaṇges* adorning *Śiva's* head is conceived almost as a royal attribute since he is an emperor among dancers. The bound up crown of *Śiva's jaṭās* is treasure house of all prosperity and auspiciousness, in which the rollicking waters of the heavenly sgtream, *Gaṅgā*, appear as a white parasol, held up by a gust from the open mouth of the terrifying Lord of snakes, with hoods expanded by the paid of being drawn into a tight knot;

payad vas sa samastamangalanidhis sambhor jatajutako
yasmin lolalasaddyumandalagalanmandakinivaribhih
gadhagranthini piditoragapatipraspharaphullataphana
bhimavyavrtavaktramarutadhrtais svetatapatrayitam[219]

---

217 Epigraphia India XXV, p. 176
218 Ibid, I, p. 307
219 Ibid, I, p. 254

A *Pallava* sculpture of *Śiva* now in the Natonal Museum, New Delhi, shows him as Alidhanrttamurti, dancing almost seated in the alidha posture, not only as the great dancer, mahanata, dancing the celebration of triumph over the Tripuras, buy also as the master who inspires others to dance. *Devī* usually dances with *Śiva*, and *Kālī* even challenged him, though she was ultimately defeated. Even *Gaṅgā* on the locks of *Śiva* turns a dancer, and in her enthusiasm throws up her wavy arms to simulate the multi - armed dancer, her lord. In her stream form, dancing above the *jaṭās* of *Śiva* she forms a canopy, not unlike a white silken umbrella, held over that presents the picture of a backdrop for the great dancer, as *Ratnākara* in his *Harāvijaya* would have it, or a malya or richly woven garland of malati flowers as *Bāṇa* would have it. It is all these suggestions that are delightfully presented in the fluttering banner - like stream of *Gaṅgā* represented on top of the panel above *Śiva's jaṭās* in an undulating wavy line giving a picture of the billows of the celestial river.

2. GAṄGĀ IS VIVID FORMS

Gaṅgā is elusive of form

Gaṅgā is elusive of form and depicted usually as a mermaid on Śiva's *jaṭās* as he dances, her body below the waist undefined and almost formless, like a tapering, wavy mass. *Bāṇa* imagines that the lower part of *Gaṅgā* suggests the disarray of her limbs as a result of her fail on *Śiva's* head :

paramesvarottamangapatadurlalitangam gaṅgām iva[220]

But the meandering stream of *Gaṅgā* is so elusive of form, that she creates a doubt in the minds of even the celestials, who find it as difficult to comprehend her physical form as her innate power to almost drown *Śiva*. The stream of Gaṅgā, with lovely tortuous waves meandering on *Śiva's* head, create doubts in the minds of the celestials as to whether they are lily garlands, digits of the moon,

220 Garsacavita VIII, p. 77

the sprouts of deeds of merit, the sloughs of snakes, or ashes falling from *Śiva*:

> *kim malah kumudasya kim sasikalah kim dharmakarmankurah*
> *kim va kancukikancukah kim atha va bhutyudagama bhantyami]*
> *ittham uakvitarkitas sivasirassancarinakapaga-*
> *ringadvalgutarangabhangitatayah punyaprapah pantu vah*[221]

Gaṅgā, kind - hearted rasamayadevi

Gaṅgā is a rasamayadevi, tender at heart in her sympathy for all, particularly the suffering. She is one with Devi, Pārvatī herself, though both are daughters of the hard, rocky mountain, Himalaya. The wonder is that both melt like snow or butter and are invariably kind. If the line from the verse describing the eye that destroyed Cupid and rejuvenated him again - *dṛśa* dagdham manasijam drsaivonmilayanti yah - refers to the eye of Śiva and the eye of *Devī*, it also refers to the eye of *Gaṅgā. Ratnākara* in any case specially supports this, as he is convinced that the kind-hearted stream that purifies and saves millions on earth, cannot be different even in the case of the most erring; and *Manmatha* only helped the charm of Devi and even that of *Gaṅgā* to be appreciated by the only one who could appreciate it, their lord *Śiva* himself, and lost his therefore.

The *Gaṇges* stream on *Śiva's* head appearing like the moon melting and dripping on the fire, suggests the extinguishing of the flame of the third eye, in which act the feminine aspect of Devi, rejuvenanting, by her tenderness, grace and spiritual beauty, the potency of Cupid, re-assures his existence, as is elsewhere also closely indicated by *Ratnākara*:

> *mandakinī sirasi maulikapalapattasamghattajarjarataranga-ghatā vibhati*
> *yasyordhvanetrasikhiviplutacandrakhanda visyandamansisra-mrtanirjharasrih*[222]

---

221 Epiyraphia Indica II. p. 10 and Corpus Inscriptionum Indicarum IV, p. 314.
222 *Haravijaya* 1, 38

Gaṅgā, a pratyaksa or visible form of Śiva

Abhinavagupta following *Kālidāsa* has accorded the highest place to *Gaṅgā* as one of the *pratyaksamūrti* or perceivable forms of *Śiva.* He equates the element of water not with its mightier receptacle, the ocean, but with the stream of the *Gaṅgā* which has, as many poets have elsewhere described, filled the ocean itself and widened it. In describing the *aṣṭamūrti* aspect, *Abhinavagupta* in his commentary on *Bharata's Naṭyaśāstra* specially describes *Gaṅgā* who dances on *Śiva's jaṭās* as his liquid form, *jalamayamurti. Abhinavagupta* devotedly invokes *Devī* herswelf, also including *Gaṅgā,* by making her sarasa, composed of stream and the gush of compassion, the acquatic form of her lord, *Śiva* himself, as she is the tender creeper springing from the seed - source of *Brahmā* who is the maker or the creator of the entire world drama in all its activity :

samsaranatyajananadhatrbijalatajusim
jalamūrtim sivam patyus sarasam paryupasmahe[223]

This closely follows *Kālidāsa*, who describes Gaṅgā as the acquatic form of *Śambhu: sambhor ambumayī* murtis saiva devi *surapaga* (*Kumārasambhava* X, 26). The same idea is given in epigraphical literature also, as in the descriptions of the *aṣṭamūrti* of *Śiva*. The likeness of *Gaṅgā* with the acquatic form of *Śiva* is clear in the expression, sarupam. The wonder is that *Śiva* and *Gaṅgā* being the same, *Śiva* still has an existence separate from *Gaṅgā*, whom he holds on his head, and this is the wonder the poet also experiences. Not only that, but including *Devī* who has her own separate existence as part of himself, *Śiva* has a third on his head, which makes for rapid ripples on the hitherto unruffled surface of his pleasant lake of family life. *Śiva* the highest, beyond whom nothing exists, is yet so tolerant as to allow a separate existence for *Gaṅgā* that could well creae disruption in the house with the quarreling among the co-wives, *Gaṅgā* and *Gaurī*:

223 Abhinavabhārati on *Nāṭyasāstra* II. 1

vivyad vayur vahnir jalam avanir indur dinakaras
cidadharas ceti ṭṛibhuvanam idam yanmayam abhut
sa vas sreyo deyat paramasuranathas suranadim
sarupam bibhranas sirasi girijaksepavisayah[224]

But this has been expressed elsewhere as the highest expediency on the part of *Śiva* who, though he is all powerful, and could reduce the universe to ashes, graciously chooses to keep the moon on his head and *Pārvatī* and *Gaṅgā* around him, the one looking with extreme displeasure at the other. This is an example of his profound knowledge of political expediency - *rajanīti. Kavīrāja* has a wonderful description of this exercise of a rajanīti by *Śiva* who allows the moon, the mountain - born *Pārvatī* and *Gaṅgā* around him though, in his infinite power, he could stomach the deadly kalakuta poison, burn *Kāma* on the apot and transform the doomsday blaze into his luminous third eye :

jirnepyutkatakalakutakavale dagdhe hathan manmathe
nite bhasurabhalanetratanutam kalpantadavanale
yas saktya samalankrtopi sasinam śṛisailajam svardhunim
dhatte kautukarajanitinipunah payat as vas śankaraḥ[225]

Gaṅgā is also most indicative of one of the principal forms of *Śiva*, and in himself, *Śiva* along with this, blends not only one iconographic form, but several almost simultanelusly. In his *Naṭarāja* aspect, it is very interesting to see a blending of certain features of the deity's other *iconographic* forms. *Gaṅgā* on his *jaṭā*, nestling as a mermaid, recxalls *Gaṅgādhara* while the prominent moon, occasionally shown on the *jaṭā*, proclaims his aspect as *Candraśekhara*. The ear ornament, different on either lobe or present only on one when it is a spiral, usual as feminine adornment, suggests the eternal *Ardhanārīśvara*. A special and noteworthy feature in the case of *Naṭarāja* is the decoration of his *jaṭās* with

224 Historical Inscriptions of Gujarat, Cāulukya, p. 104 and Epigraphia Indica II, 440.

225 *Subhasitakóa* IV, 41

peacock feathers, at once recalling the *Kirāta* theme, in which form *Śiva* appears before *Arjuna*.

Gaṅgā fondly approaches Śiva, then recedes in fear

Gaṅgā, as the sculptor has fashioned and represented her on the *jaṭās* of *Śiva*, has sometimes been conceived as a fond companion in life, conscious of the overpowering personality of her lord, but yet anxious to whispere in his ears, unheard by Pārvatī, her whisper being more here amazement. In a beautiful metal figure of *Naṭrāja* at *Siyali* there is clearly indicated the inspiration of a tradition of faith and devotion of the baby saint *Tirujnanasambanda* associated with this village. The figure of *Gaṅgā*, here almost crawling on the *jaṭā* of *Śiva* appears to whisper in the ear of her Lord her devotional hymns, as she watches his dance and appreciates it as the most elegant.

On the other hand, in another image also in metal from Pungandur now in the Madras Museum, *Gaṅgā* is depicted as moving away towards the end of the *jaṭā*, almost afraid of the violent swirl of *Śiva's* locks as he dances his *tanḍava*. This cannot but recall another sculpture, that of *Gajanṭaka* from *Darasuram*, where even according to the indication of the dhyana text itself, the goddess *Pārvatī* herself, with the child *Skanda* on her hip, is moving away in fear, so to speak at the violent dance of her lord.

Gaṅgā and the jaṭās

In the arrangement of *Śiva's* hair itself, the sculptor has ever made it an important point not to loosen the entire bundle of locks and allow them to swiri all around, nor is the whole dressed in *makuta* fashion, as is normal in all other forms expect that of Naṭeśa. A portion of the *jaṭās* is skillfully arranged as a makuta, while the rest is allowed to fall loosely on the shoulders or back or to spread out on either side laterally, almost creating an impression of waves. This is very important as the waqvy *jaṭās* along with the moving reptiles with flowers dotted on them, create an illusion of the heavenly river as a fluttering silken flag. Are they the undulating waves of the heavenly stream? The wavy line so charmingly manipulated by the artist is certainly suggestive of the *taranga* or wave vollowing in and out, creating a sequence of undulations that not only suggest beauty but also scintillating life. Beauty is never indolent, it is dynamic. Waves never move singly, but in quick succession and create a series of charming, rolling undulations. So too, the curly hair in taranga fashion. In fact the word taranga itself means wavy. The suggestion is that the *jaṭās* of Śiva that whirl all around and undulate in wavy patterns assume the form of streams moving raidly in eddy and whirlpool, now and again changing their course if necessary, to create serpentine configurations in their flow, thereby adding charm to a combination of identical patterns of curves. Casually, *Gaṅgā*, *bhujaṅga* and *taraṅga* combine and merge for a common effect, a dazzling net of flowers on a fast-moving stream running in all directions and forming, as already remarked, a backdrop for the *Mahanata*, the great dancer, *Śiva.*

A. Gaṅgā is Purifier

Gaṅgā purifies thought and expression

In a terracotta from *Ahicchatra* representing *Śiva* as *Daksiṇāmūrti*, the form more favoured in the South, in North India, *Lakuliśa* generally takes the place of *Daksiṇāmūrti* there is a beautiful representation of *Gaṅgā* standing beside *Śiva* the Teacher. As the expo under of the highest philosophy and thought, *Śiva* wears vastra *yajnopavita* and is seated undere the Banyan tree, symbolic of expanse and shelter. It is vast knowledge that assures a cool shade from the burning glare of all illusory *tapa*, and *Śiva* as *Daksiṇāmūrti* never has Devī beside him. He is represented in this aspect almost as an ascetic, but this is only confined to *Medha, Jnāna* - or *Yogadaksiṇāmūrti*. It is only *Gaṅgā* whose presence is suggestive of purification who can stand beside him. There is an ancient belief in India that the immaculate waters of knowledge wash away the impurities of ignorance. The prayer to *Pāṇini* makes this clear :

> *yena dhauta girah pumsam vimalais sabdararibhiḥ*
> *tamas cajnanajam bhinnam tasmai paninaye namaḥ*

Śiva himself as the great Teacher taught *Pāṇini* the essence of the science of language, and in his turn *Pāṇini* purified speech itself. *Gaṅgā's* presence indicates how immaculate the divine stream is and how she removes all dress and renders pure even the thoughts and expressions of *Ṛṣis* who symbolize all created beings, celestial or terrestrial. Here again the presence of *Gaṅgā* is significant.

Gaṅgā, the only purifier in Kali

The efficacy of Gaṅgā is clearly stated in the *Mahābhārata*. Bathing anywhere in the Gaṅgā is as good as setting foot on theholy soil of *Kurukṣetra*. There is a special sanctity, however, in bathing at *Kanakhala* and *Prayaga*. But the purity of *Gaṅgā* is of special importance because she is the one holy stream, efficacious even in *Kaliyuga* which is rampant with sin and folly. In the golden age or *Kṛtayuga*, there is nothing which is unholy and nothing that requires purification and every place is a *tīrtha*, but in *Treta*, the silver age, *Puṣkara* in Rajasthan is the sacred spot that removes all sins. In Dvapara or the Copper Age, Kuruksetra is holy; but in the dark, iron age of *Kali*, it is *Gaṅgā*, the river from heaven, who purifies all. The mere utterance of the name of *Gaṅgā* purifies a sinner. A sight of the river showers all auspiciousness. A bath in the stream or a sip of her water purifies seven generations of ancestors and descendants. The moment the bone relies of anyone touch the water to the Gaṅgā, the soul is transported to heaven. There is a saying that there is no tirtha more sacred than the water of *Gaṅgā* and no God higher than *Keśava*:

> *sarvam krtayuge punyam tretayam puskaram smṛtaṁ*
> *dvapare'pi kuruksetram gaṅgā kaliyuge smrta*
> *yavadasthi manusyasya gaṅgāyas sprsate jalam*
> *tavat sa puruso rajan svargaloke mahiyate*
> *na gaṅgāsadrsam tirtham na devah kesavat parah.*[226]

---

226 *Mahābhārata* 3, 85, 90, 94 and 96.

Immanence of Gaṅgā: Bāṇagaṅgā issuing from the tip of the arrow

When *Bhiṣma* lay on his bed of arrows on the battlefield at *Kuruksetra*, he felt thirsty and asked for water. The several princes that were attending on him, including *Duryodhana* and others, rushed hither and thithere to quickly obtain water from the nearest available spot, but the wise Arjuna fulfilled his wish immediately by shooting his arrow deep into the earth to bring out a jet of water, that spurted out and quenched *Bhiṣma*'s thirst. This illustrates the omnipresence of the nearly always invisible form of *Gaṅgā*, the pure stream used not only to moisten the lips but also to purify the holy one on his deathbed. This is symbolically repeated even today when a ladle of Gaṅgā water is poured into the mouth of a dying person assuring him salvation and bliss. This jet of water drawn from the depths of the earth by Arjuna as *Bhiṣma* lay on a bed of arrows is a favourite theme in miniature painting and is one of the five pictures in Pancaratnagitā:

avidhyat prthivim parthah parsve bhismasya daksine
utpapata tato dhara varino vimala subha
sitasyamrtakalpasya divya gandharasasya ca
atarpayat tatah parthas sitaya jaladharaya[227]

Bhīṣma, the son of Gaṅgā, was blessed in this way by his mother as he died. The story goes that when *Gaṅgā* learnt that *Bhīṣma* was lying on the bed of arrows after resolving to die only in uttarayana, she sent to him the holy *Ṛṣis* on her banks in the form of swans, symbols of immaculate life and thought. The *Ṛṣis* blessed him with power to live on till the sun returned to the northern course, *uttarāyana*, which would be the most auspicious moment for his casting off the mortal coil :

uttarayanam anvicchan bhīsmah kurupitamahah
tasya tanmatamajnaya Gaṅgā himavatas suta
maharsin hamsarupena presayamasa tatra vai[228]

---

227 *Mahābhārata* 6, 121, 24-25

228 *Mahābhārata* 6, 119, 97-98.

B. Mother, Sustainer and Daughter

Gaṅgā, a river goddess and mother

Gaṅgā though not essentially different from other streams in India, is however considered the one and only holy stream that almost represents all the rest The concept of the river in India is that of a sustaining mother. The stream of the river carries payas. The word *pāyas* stands for both water and milk. Appropriately this has been used in relation to the river as the stream that sustains the people, her children, with water, as a mother sustains her babies with her milk. This idea is uppermost in the mind of every poet, and *Kālidāsa* calls *Gaṅgā samanyādhātrī*, a mother for the entire area she flows through. As *Rāma* approaches *Ayodhya* in his aerial car and sights *Sarayū*, he addresses *Sītā* and describes the river in affectionate terms as if she were his mother beckoning and trying to embrace him with here wavy arms :

> *seyam madiya jananiva tena manyena rajna Sarayur viyukta*
> *dure vasantam sisiranilair mam tarangahastair upaguhativa*[229]

On her lap, the children of the soil could sit and muse without thought of the future, as the region known as nadi-matrika was sustained by the river :

> *yam saikatotsangasukhocitanam prajyaih payobhih*
> *parivardhi-tanam*
> *samanyadhatrim iva manasam me sambhavayatyuttarakosa-*
> *lanam*[230]

Gaṅgā as sustainer

Why is it that the Gaṅgā is depicted on both door jambs of temples in South India? The reason is not far to seek. Gaṅgā is the most important river, she is the model for all others, and naturally she alone is repeated. We find that the river goddess on the makara which typifies the Gaṅgā is represented as early as the second

---

229 *Raghuvaṁsa* xiii, 63.

230 Ibid. xiii, 52.

century A.D. on a slab at *Amarāvatī*; she is repeated here as in later sculpture, and two identical figures of the river goddess flank a *Nāga*. The original slab is now in the British Museum. Here the goddess is shown carrying food and water in a tray and a jug respectively, and resembles exactly a similar figure of Kausana date, without the vehicle, in the Bharat Kala Bhavan at Banaras. This attitude of the goddess suggesting abundant water and food obtained by a plentiful harvest of splendid crops raised without the least effort in the riverirrigated area, reminds us of the line by *Bhāravi* in the context of the peace and plenty of the *Kuru* realm, watered by the *Yamunā* and the *Gaṅgā* that assure crops without tail:

sukhena labhya dadhatah krisvalair
akrstapacya iva sasyasampadah
vitanrati ksemam adevamatrikas
ciraya tasmin kuravas cakasati[231]

This sculpture is a visual commentary on the term *nadīmaṭrkā* which is the same as *adeamaṭrkā*, as opposed to *devamaṭrkā*.

Following the description of Nadīdevata in the *Viṣṇudharmottara*, which records the traditional concept of the river goddess, there are carvings in *Amarāvatī* that show her carrying a *purṇakumbha* or a vessel brimming wikth water. The *purṇakumbha* itself, with lotuses and water, is a symbol not only of plenty and auspiciousness but also of the river, and the earliest symbolic representation of the purifying influence of the river goddess, guarding the temple entrance on either side, which accounts for the presence of *purṇakumbhas* flanking the doorway:

pragdraravedivinivesitapurṇakumbham[232]

C. *Gaṅgā*, symbol of purity

Of all rivers, Gaṅgā has always had the highest appeal. Her sacred name is on the lips of every Hindu and the sincere belief is that mere

231 *Kirātārjunīya* i, 17.
232 *Raghuvaṁśa* v, 63.

utterancde of her name purifies one. She is the heavenly river that the earth was fourunate enough to receive when brought by the great efforts of an indefatigable chain of princes for the purification not only of their ancestors' ashes but of one and all. It is the standard by which the greatness of every other river is judged, as the *Gaṅgā* stands supreme among all others. A number of other rivers such as the *Kāverī*, are believed to be transformed into the *Gaṅgā* at least for a few days in the year. At any rate, this is the faith that inspires pilgrims who dip in the river on those sacred days specified in the *Purāṇas*.

Gaṅgā and Yamunā as dvārapālikas purify visitors

As one enters the gopura of any temple in South India, one may see on either side of the door jamb a figure of *Gaṅgā* standing on a *Makara* and holding a creeper that issues from its mouth. This proceeds in a meandering fashion to form circles that frame panels and represent different forms of deities and figures of dancers that run in a line up to the lintel, several 'feet in height. *Gaṅgā's* presence purifies the visitor as he enters. One may wonder why *Gaṅgā* is repeated on the makara twice, once on either side, and why she of all other rivers should have been chosen for representation when other rivers such as the *Godāvarī*, the *Kṛṣṇavenī* and the *Kāverī* are there to choose from. The obvious reason is that Gaṅgā is considered to holiest. To see why *Gaṅgā* is so represented in sculpture, it will be necessary to look at Gupta sculpture, especially that on temple door jambs. Gaṅgā and *Yamunā* are represented in human form on temple door jambs almost invariably. The rivers stand on their respective vehicles, the *makrānā* and the *kacchapa*, *crocodile* and *tortoise*, waited on by their attendants - a maid raising an umbrella over *Gaṅgā's* head and maid carrying *Yamunā's* wallet *Swans* that *flutter* above with garlands of lotuses and lilies in their beaks, evoke cool, fragrant and acquatic associations. The fluttering *Vidyādharas* above holding garlands suggest the highest honour and reverence that even the celestials have for the river goddess. Some times botht rivere goddesses carry water jars, as they should do, according to the *silpa* texts that describe their *iconography*, as for instance in the *Viṣṇudharmottara*. Even *Gaṅgā* in human form reminds us at once of *Kālidāsa's* description of rivers in *anthropomorphic* form attending on *Śiva*.

A very fine representation of *Gaṅgā* and *Yamunā* guarding the doorway comes from *Dah Paravatīya* in Assam. A similar one from Buxar in Bihar in the Indian Museum is also interesting. The *sārasa* birds fluttering over the head of the river goddess, as though fascinated by the sweet notes of the titny, jingling, golden beads of her girdle, present a picture like that painted by *Kālidāsa* of similar birds on the wing ever the stream of the *Godāvarī*:

amur vimānantaralambininaṁ
surtva svanam kancanakinkininaṁ
pratyudvrajantiva kham utpatantyo
godāvarī arasapanktayas tvaṁ[233]

D. Gaṅgā as an adornament for the earth

In the mind of the Gupta and *Vakāṭaka* sculptor, and even in earlier centuries, it is the *ekāvalī* composed of fine pearls that was preferred among necklets and this preference often expresses itself through the brush and chisel in painting and carving; in representations of the *Gaṅgā* and the *Yamunā* the same ekāvalī is shown to beautify the neck. In picturesque fashion Kālidāsa presents the pure white stream of the *Gaṅgā* gradually narrowing in size in the distant landscape, as a necklace of pearls closely fitting the earth damsel's neck :

eṣa prasannastimitapravāha
sarid vidūrantarabhavatanvi
mandākinī bhati nagopakanthe
muktāvalī kanthagateva bhūmeh[234]

---

233 *Raghuvaṁśa* xiii, 33
234 *Raghuvaṁśa* xiii, 48

E. The commingling of Gaṅgā and Yamunā

The Gupta sculptor was as fascinated with the beauty of the mingling of the colours of the *Gaṅgā* and *Yamunā* in the confluence at *Prayāga*, as *Kālidāsa* himself, whose fancy brings both streams close enough even before they commingle, to create an optical illusion. The beauty of the white stream of *Gaṅgā* enhanced by the commingling of the blue waters of the *Yamunā* stirs *Kālidāsa*'s fancy into suggesting that the white sandal paste from the breasts of the damsels in the *Śurasena* king Susena's *harem* washed off during their sportive baths, makes *Yamunā* look as if she were charged with the waters of the *Gaṅgā*, even near Mathura:

yasyavarodhastanacandananaṁ
praksalanad variviharakale
kalindakanya mathuram gatāpī
gaṇgormisamsaktajaleva bhatī[235]

Appayya Diksita in his *Kuvalayanandā* gives just the opposite picture of how the colyrium from the eyes of the damsels of the *Mālavā* king's enemies had made the stream of *Narmadā* dark, and consequently created a misapprehension in the mind of *Samudrarāja*, the lord of the rivers :

kalindi bruhi kumbhodbhava jaladhir aham nama grhnasī
kasma
cchatror me narmadaham tvaṁ api vadasi me nama kasmat
sapatnyah
malinyam toorhi kasmad anubhavasī milatkajjalair malavinaṁ
netrambhobhih kim asam samajani kupitah
kuntalaksonipalaḥ[236]

The most glorious picture in literature of the commingling of rivers is that of the *Gaṅgā* and *Yamunā* by *Kālidāsa*. This picturesque confluence at *Prayāga* has made it a great *tīrtha*, and *Kālidāsa's* description is a painting in words, like the masterpiece of the sculptor

235 *Raghuvaṁśa* vi, 48
236 Kuvalayanandā

which has glorified the tirtha by representing the rivers personified on their streams which commingle and flow to meet *Samudrarāja*, as depicted in the *Udayagiri* cave in Central India.

The confluence of these two rivers that arrests attention both by its natural charm and aesthetic appeal as well as its sanctity, is probably unrivalled. The confluences of several rivers that become sacred spots, are known by the appellation, tirtha; even individual rivers can become tirthas, and their water is purifying in effect: I *tirthajalani kaccit.* The *tīrtha* was so highly revered and played such an important role in the life of man in ancient India, that it stands to reason that there should be, wherever possible, a visual representation of one of the most outstanding of its kind in India; the importance of *Prayāga* being what it is, it is represented in one of the earliest Gupta sculptures. The confluence at Prayaga is sanctified in the *Purāṇas*, deep-rooted in faith, and a hallowed spot for pilgrimage from all over the subcontinent. The most important description in literature and undoubtedly the most picturesque of the commingling of rivers, that of *Gaṅgā* and *Yamunā*, is given by t he sweetest of poets, *Kālidāsa.* Yonder flows Gaṅgā witht her stream broken by the wavelets of *Yamunā*, appearing here like a necklace of pearls interspersed with spphires shedding lusture, there like a garland of white lotuses with blue lilies woven into it at intervals; sometimes like the row of white swans fond of the *Mānasa* lake touching the dark swans, elsewhere like decorative creeper patterns painted in dark *Aguru* paste on sandal background for the earth; somewhere like the moonlight mottled by dark patches of shade here and there, elsewhere like a line of spotless autumnal clouds with the sky seen through the interstices; and somewhyyere like the body of *Śiva* smeared with ashes and decorated with black serpents. This glorious confluence of rivers with an effect in colour realized visually and not easily expressed in words, has been most vividly expressed by the great poet in his verses :

kvacit prabhālepibhir indrānīlair
muktamayi yastir ivanuviddha

anyatra mala sitapankajanam
indivarair utkhacitantareva
kvacit khaganam priyamanasanam
kadambasamsargavativa panktih
anyatra kalagurudattapatra
bjaktir bhuvas candanakalpiteva
kvacit prabha candramasi tamobhis
chayavilinais sabalikrteva
anyatra subhra saradabhralekha
randhresvivalaksyaanabhahp;radesa
kvacit ca krsnoragabhusaneva
bhasmangaraga tanur iśvarasya
pasyanavadyangi vibhati gaṅgā
bhinnapravaha yamunatarangaih[237]

In the next verse,

samudrapatnyor jalasannipate
putatmanam atra kilabnhisekat
tatvavabodhena vinapi bhuyas
tanutyajam nasti sarirabandhah[238]

The sanctity of the confluence of the two rivers is clearly stated, for a bath in the holy water is more efficacious than even the attainment of supreme knowledge which assures release from the bondage of birth and death and immortality. The sacred *ksetṛa*, the greatest among holy spots in India visited by pilgrims and eulogized by *Kālidāsa*, has been presented graphically in sculpture in thecaved at *Udayagiri* in Central India in the vicinity of Mahavaraha. *Viṣṇu* raised *Pṛthvī* from the ocean and served as the model for the great Gupta kings who rescued the earth and their own families and raised their royal glory to heights worthy of their prowess. In this context and scene *Samudra* is personified as carrying a ratnakalasa to suggest that he is Ratnakara. The rivers flow into the ocean, the streams

237 *Raghuvaṁśa* xiii, 54-57.
238 *Raghuvaṁśa* xiii, 58.

are shown commingling their waters with it. The two principal holy rivers, *Gaṅgā* and *Yamunā*, are shown standing in human form, each on her own vehicle and on their own streams which join and proceed to meet the ocean, also personified, that stands to receive them. There is music, dance and festivity as the pilgrims bathe. The result of this bath, *immortality*, gained by becoming a divine being, is suggested by the immortals fluttering above the stream. This is a vivid picture of a great *tīrtha*, probably the most important in India, and the only one that has been so effectively represented in sculpture.

Gaṅgā, daughter of the mountain king, Himavān

Himalāya typifies nobility as a lofty, unswerving and massive object, great and unparalleled glacier that he is. He is the lord of all mountains: *Himālaya nama nāgādhirājah*. That is why he is considered the motionless form of Viṣṇu himself : *sthāne tvaṁ sthavaratmanaṁ viṣṇum ahus tathā hi te*[239]. Very often, the mountain is called the father of *Gaurī: padas taṁ bbhito nisannahariṇa gauriguroh paranah* (*Abhijnānaśākuntalam* vi, 18). *Himavan* who is mighty, auspicious, noble and majestic, is also holy, but even he, the motionless aspect of *Viṣṇu*, is rendered more holy by the *Gaṅgā* flowing from his crest. He is conscious of this fact when he specially makes this remark as he welcomes the seven holy sages, *sapta ṛṣis,* who approach him for the betrothal of *Umā* with *Śiva*:

> *avaimi putam atmanam dvayenaiva dvijottamah*
> *murdhni gaṅgāprapatena dhautapadambhasa ca vah*[240]

Just as *Gaṅgā* is proud of her origin in the foot of Viṣṇu, so is she equally proud of her consequent origin from the crest of *Himālaya*. This doubly assures the noblest *abhijātya*, birth of the highest consequence :

> *yathaiva slaghyate Gaṅgā padena paramesthināḥ*
> *prabhāvena dvitiyena tathaivocchirasa tvāya*[241]

---

239 *Kumārasambhava*, vi, 72.

240 *Kumārasambhara,* vi, 57.

241 *Kumārasambhava,* vi, 70.

F. Gaṅgā as Suranimnaga

Before descending on the crest of Himavan or even on the *jaṭās* of Śiva, Gaṅgā flowed as the river of the celestials. In this special aspect she has her own characteristic like *Surabhi* or the divine cow, that rests under the shade of the *Kalpaka* tree, asit *kalpatarucchāyām asrita surabhih pathi, s*ince *Gaṅgā* also flows past the *kalpavṛkṣa*. An anthropomorphic form of *Gaṅgā* is represented in a *Sena sculpture,* standing under the *kalpavṛkṣa* and holding, as a river goddess should, a *purṇakumbha* or a brimming vessel in her hand, suggestive of the abundance of her holy water. This beautiful sculpture of the Eastern Indian medieval school is undoubtedly one of the best representations of *Gaṅgā*, and significantly also a suggestive one, indicating the celestial association of the river Suraṅiṁnāga.

G. Jāhnavī Gaṅgā or the daughter of Jahnu

At Ellora the appellation *Jahnoh kanyām* of *Kālidāsa* has a pictorial commentary as it were, as the panel here is not of *Gaṅgādharamūrti* but of *Gaṅgāvisarjanamūrti*, Śiva releasing *Gaṅgā* from his locks at the earnest request of *Bhagīratha*. Here *Gaṅgā* an pride, descending torrentially onto the locks of *Śiva*, and subsequently humbled, is seen imprisoned in the cage of locks for a number of years.[242] It was only after *Bhagīratha's* desperate entreaties that she was released again.

This time, as the stream followed *Bhagīratha* she devastated the hermitage of the sage *Jāhnu* on the way and so enraged him that in one gulp he swallowed up the mighty river, to the utter dismay of *Bhagīratha* who, this time, had to entreat the sage to release the river again. As the sage graciously obliged him, the river Gaṅgā was allowed to flow out again through his ear, and ever since, the ear has been considered the birth place of *Gaṅgā*; even in *Sandhyā* the ear is touched in lieu of washing the hand. Issuing from the ear of the sage *Jāhnu* she became the daughter of

242 Dr Sivaramamurti C, op cit. p. 65

Jāhnu, *Jāhnavī*, and it is as *Jāhnavī* that she flowed again towards where *Bhagīratha* led her to wash the ashes of his ancestors. In the sculpture from *Pattadakal* as at *Ellora* the sage *Jāhnu* is shown seated sippling *Gaṅgā* as she issued from *Śiva's* locks, releasing her through the ear.

H. Gaṅgā as Tṛisṛotas

At *Elephanta* there is a marvelous panel representing Śiva as *Gaṅgādhara*, but here the sculptor is not satisfied with a tame representation of just a mermaid - like figure for the river. The three streams of *Gaṅgā* as she flows in heaven, on earth and in the netherworld, in which aspects she is *Tṛipāthagā* and *Trisroṭas*, are delineated as the three faces of the meremaid on the locks of *Śiva*. They also suggest the *Triveṇī* or the three streams, *Gaṅgā* with *Yamunā* and *Sarasvatī* that join and swell her waters, further sanctifying the already sacred stream of the heavenly river. This is an outstanding sculptural rendering of the *Triveṇī* aspect of *Gaṅgā* in a *Gaṅgādhara* panel.

I. Gaṅgā as Tṛipāthagā

The greatest glory of *Gaṅgā* is that she is the one river to be singled out for representation. She has three streams, she flows in three regions and she purifies three different areas, *Kālidāsa* delights in often referring to *Gaṅgā*, the stream as she flkows in heaven as *Akāsagaṅgā*, where in the elephants of the eight quarters bathe with delight and the seven *Ṛṣis* perform their holy ablutions:

> *nadatyakasagaṅgāya srotasyuddamadiggaje*[243]
> *and*
> *aplutas tiramandarakusumotkiravicisu vyomagaṅgāpravahesu dingnāgamadagandhiśu*[244]

The presence of *Gaṅgā* in *Pātāla* was a matter of necessity as *Bhagīratha's* ancestors who pursued the sacrificial horse were

243 *Raghuvaṁśa* i, 78.

244 *Kumārasambhava* vi, 5.

cursed there. *Gaṅgā*, who with her cool breeze and the shade of *Mandāra* trees on her bank, served as the ideal pleasure ground for divine beings:

mandakinyas salilasisirais sevyamana marudbhir
mandaranam anutataruham chayaya varaitosnah[245]

trickled down from *Śiva's* locks on which she had fallen, and following *Bhagīratha*, reached the ashes of his ancestors in the netherworld to take them by the efficacy of her purificatory power and step by step, as on a ladder, to heaven:

jahnoh kanyām sāgaratanayasvargasopanapanktim[246]

Gaṅgā as *Tṛipāthāga*, the sacred river purifying the three worlds, is the theme of a sculptural narration on a pillar in the *Virupāksa* temple at *Paṭṭadakal*. Here is represented her great spirit of self sacrifice and kind compliance with the wishes of the *Vasus* whom she delivered from thecurse of *Vaśiṣṭha*, and her efforts to wash the remains of and raise to heaven, the sons of *Sagara* who were burnt by sage *Kapila*, whom they attempted to attack for carrying away their sacrificial horse, as they supposed by the presence of the animal in his vicinity in *Pātāla*. The netherworld is indicated by the diggaja supporting the earth, and the sixty thousand princes who rushed as one against *Kapila* are suggested in one aggressive figure attacking a sage; the approach of *Gaṅgā* is, as in the other panels, suggested both by a stgream and by her anthropomorphic form as a damsel.

Her descent to earth is depicted in the panel where the stream and the maiden representing it, approach *Śiva* who receives her on his locks and imprisons her there. Once again on the strength of *Bhagīratha's* prayers and serere *penance* the stream of *Gaṅgā* is released and proceeds towards the mountain *Himavan*, whence she flows down past sage *Jāhnu's* hermitage where the enranged

245 *Meghadūta* ii, 6.
246 *Meghadūta* i, 50.

anchorite receives her in his *kamanḍalu* and swallows her in one gulp. Again on the entreaties of *Bhagīratha* she is released through the ear of the sage, to finally reach the ashes of the sons of *Sagara* in the netherworld.

The description of how *Kuśa*, when he approached Gaṅgā on his way to *Ayodhya* from *Kusavatī* to re-establish it as his capital, bowed to theholy river whose waters conducted to the world of immortals, the remains of his ancestors who were reduced to ashes bby thhe anger of *Kapila*, suggests the veneration due to this great river. Even *Kuśa*, the very image of his father who was the great incarnation of the Lord Himself, bowed to her with devotion :

sa purvajanam kapilena rosad
bhasmavasesikrtavigarahanaṁ
suralayapraptinimittam aṁbhas
traisrotasam naaululitam vavande[247]

In a panel depicting *Gandhāra* in the *Śiva* temple built by the mighty *Çola* emperor, *Rājendra* at *Gaṅgāikonḍācolapuraṁ*, this story of *Bhagīratha's* penance is clearly illustrated. *Gaṅgā* was revered so much by this mighty monarch that he brought the water of thesacred river down to the south in vessels offered as tribute by kings overcome by him in battle in the region of the river. A large lake dug for this purpose was the 'liquid pillar of victory', and he assumed the title '*Gaṅgāikoṇḍacola*', the *Çola* who brought the *Gaṅgā*. The central panel in the niche depicts Śiva appenssing Pārvatī who is vexed with him and consequently turns her face away, distressed at the prospect of a *co-wife* in *Gaṅgā* who has settled on the locks of *Śiva*. At *Lepāksī* there is a painting that graphically renders this quarrel in *Śiva's* household in the vivid picture he presents of how *Gaṅgā* clutched at *Śiva's* locks with her wavy hands laughing through her waters at Pārvatī's angry face :

tasmad gaccher anukanakhalam sailarajavatirnam
jahnoh kanyam sāgaratauayasvargasopana panktim

247 *Raghuvaṁśa* xvi, 35.

gaurivaktrabhrukutiracanam ya rihasyeva phenais
sambhoh kesagrahanam akarod indulagnormihasta[248]

The carvings on either side of the panel show the penance of *Bhagīratha* and his determined effort to bring the *Gaṅgā* from heaven, a determination which has become proverbial on account of its almost impossible nature. However mighty and torrential *Gaṅgā* may have been, and we know according to the story that the came down with great force expecting Śiva to collapse under the great torrent, she was, nevertheless, lost in his profusion of locks.

In sculptures *Gaṅgā* is therefore depicted as approaching *Śiva* humbly. In carvings representing *Gaṅgādhara* in South India and the Deccan and also at *Elephanta*, *Gaṅgā* on the locks of *Śiva* is represented in true acquatic fashion as a mermaid. One or two locks of *Śiva* singled out and held lightly to receive the mighty torrent, show how easy was this sport for the Lord who could swallow the poison, *Kālakuta*, no less easily. At *Tirucirapalli*, in the *Pallava* cave, the Gaṅgādhara panel represents the simple case with which *Gaṅgā* was received by *Śiva.* The finest representation of *Gaṅgā* in mermaid fashion is probably found in the temple of *Dārasuram* and in this the wavy line decoration on the lower part of the figure suggests beautifully the form of the heavenly river.[249]

The blessed life on the banks of the Gaṅgā

Dwelling on the banks of the river Gaṅgā is a privilege. Sanskrit rhetoricians take a delight in explaining the line *gaṅgāyaṁ ghosah* as suggesting pleasant cool, breezes and a purifying atmosphere, saitya *pavanadī.* But it is not the proximity of thte *Gaṅgā* alone that is believed to have this purifying effect. Even from a great distance the very utterance of the name is enough for the attainment of final bliss:

Gaṅgā gaṇgeti yo bruyad yojanānāṁ satairapi
vimuktas sarvapapebhyo Viṣṇulokam sa gacchati.

---

248 *Meghadūta* i, 50.

249 Dr. Śivaramamurti C., op. cit. p. 77.

The sanctity of the *Gaṅgā* and the blessed life on her banks where gods, sages, men, birds and animals alike throng, is most vividly represented in the *Mahābalipuraṁ* scene of *Arjuna's penance* on her banks near the mountain *Raivataka*. We have only to glance at the description of the heavenly river in the *Kumārasambhava* to understand the sculpture more clearly.

At *Kālidāsa* has drawn attention to aloka, *avagaha* and *ācamana* by the celestials, we find in this significant sculpture all the Devas, including *Sūrya, Candra, Siddhas*, *Vidyādharas, Yaksas, Kinnaras* and *Nāgas* approaching *Gaṅgā* from both sides. Gaṅgā herself is to be imagined as the stream in the cleft between the two rocks which are carved and, at the supposed location of the stream, there are *Nāgas* and *Nāginīs* to suggest water. That the stream flows from heaven to the earth is suggested by the many celestials in the upper region. Lower down, *Ṛṣis* and *Munikumāras* and a shrine for Viṣṇu suggest the *Gaṅgā* flowing on the earth. At the lowest point the Nāgas and the *Diggajas* suggest the netherworld where also she flows:

tribhis srotobhirasrantam punana bhuvanatrayam[250]

and

subhrari abhramkasair urmisatais svarganivasinam
kathayantim ivalokavaghacamanadikam
susnatanam munindranam balikarmocitairalam
bahis puspotkaraih kirnatiram durvaksatanvitaih
brahmadhyanaparair yogaparabrahmasanasthitaih
yoganidragatair yogapattabandhair upasritam
padangusthagrabhumisthais suryasambaddhadrstibhih
brahmarsibhih param Brahmā grnadbhir upasevitam[251]

The *Ṛṣis* engaged in meditation on the banks of the *Gaṅgā* are shown ilk exactly the same position as *Kālidāsa* has described them, some in *brahmāsana*, in *brahmādhyana* and *yoganidrā*, with

250 *Kumārasambhava* x, 31.

251 *Kumārasambhava* x, 44-47.

the *yogapatta*, a strip of cloth bound round their legs, and some, like *Arjuna* and *Munikumāra*, with their eyes turned towards the sun. *Arjuna* is depicted as an ascetic standing on his toe and doing severe penance. The *Munikumāra* is performing the *suryopasthana* after his *Sandhyā*, with his hands and fingers clasped in *yamapasamudra*, to look at the sun through the aperture so formed. The bath preceding the *Sandhyā* is indicated by another *Munikumāra* wringing wtater from his clothes. Yet another Munikumara carries a vessel of water suggesting bali and *pujā* during the course of which flowers and *aksatas* are strewn about. This atmosphere of devotion has helped opposites like lion and deer, cat and mouse to come together, and the cat has so changed his habits that, instead of his usual *biḍalavṛata*, he actually stands up in *penance*, like the most rigorous anchorite answering to the description :

> *saraganvayanirvanakarini dharamadharini*[252]

J. Gaṅgā, the principal stream in the Triveṇī

One of the most important sculptural groups representing the rivers is from *Ellora* and it is unique as it portrays not only the two famous visible ones, *Gaṅgā* and *Yamunā*, but the triple stream that makes the great *sangama* at *Triveṇī*. The three great rivers are shown as three goddesses in *anthropomorphic* form. This representation of personified rivers, expecially those that compose the great *Prayāgaksetra*, is important when we consider that such a stress is laid on them only in one other place, *Udayagiri*, where however the invisible river is omitted.

The sanctity of *Sarasvatī*, as she flows in the vicinity of the holy *Kuruksetra*, is evident in the verse used by *Mammata* in his book on rhetoric to illustrate *yamaka* or alliteration :

> *Sarasvatī prasādam me sthitim cittasarasvatī*
> *sara svatī kuru ksetrakuruksetrasarasvatī*[253]

252 *Kumārasambhava* x, 30.

253 *Kāvyaprakāśa* ix, 366.

The mind is here conceived of as being as pure as *Kuruksetra*, and the blessing of *Saraswatī*, the Goddess of Leaning, by her presence in the mind, is as efficacious as the holy presence of this pure stream in the sacred soil of *Kuruksetra*.

In fact, during the daily bath, every *Hindu* addresses the principal rivers and invokes their presence in the water. The same invocation to the rivers *Gaṅgāa, Yamunā, Sarasvatī, Godavari, Narmada, Śindhu* and *Kāverī* is used while bathing the images of household deities during the daily *pujā*. The influence of the rivers, like that of the Indian mind. It leapt with joy, as towards the mother, at the very sight of every one of these holy streams, and it is no wonder that they sight of every one of these holy streams, and it is no wonder thtat they are honoured with the best of poetry and art. Yet invoking all the rivers, the one stream that is always uppermost in the mind is *Gaṅgā*. That is why a few drops of this holy stream, are poured into the lips of one's nearest and dearest on his deathbed as an assurance of liberation. And again, afrter cremation, the remains are brought from every nook and corner of the country only to be immersed in the Ganges, the one stream that takes the front rank among all the rest.

The sanctity of *Gaṅgā* is such that all sins vanish the moment a drop from the stream touches the body. It is the realization of this that almost restrained Appayya Diksita in his sudden critical remark at *Jagannnātha*, enjoying the company of his *Yavani* consort in thestory of the imaginary meeting between the two. This is anything but a historical fact. Diksita is supposed to have remarked

kim nissamkam sese sesevayasī samagate mṛtyau
athava sukhaṁ sayitha nikate jagarti jāhnavi jananī.

He suddently cuts himself short by saying, 'I am sorry for my remark but it appears rather to be the other way about. Very close to you, mother *Gaṅgā* is quite alive to the situation.' It is as much as to say that *Gaṅgā* herself has permitted her beloved son, *Jagannātha*, to behave as he likes and who is Diksita to question her decision? The story goes that *Gaṅgālaharī*, the famous and beautiful humn on *Gaṅgā*, was composed by him almost immediately in a spirit of remorse, and legend has it that the stream of the *Gaṅgā* mounted up the steps, one by one as the verses were composed, till finally, as he completed them, she washed away both Jagannātha and his consort into her stream, granting them eternal union and liberation from the bonds of birth and death true to the spirit of sympathy and forgiveness characteristic of a mother. She is prepared to excuse even the heinous crime of a child. For is it not true, as *Śankara* says, that a wicked boy there may be, but not a wicked mother:

kuputro jayeta kvacid api kumata na bhavatī.

Gaṅgā's purity is such that almost everywhere her sanctity is claimed in some stream or pool in different places. *Vijayaksetra*, *Nandiksetra* and *Varāhakṣetra* in Kashmir are described as places hallowed by *Viṣṇu*, where the famous *Mandapakṣetra* and *Uttaramānasa* are located. Here heinous sins are washed away even as the pilgrim approaches:

gaccha kasmiran papanasanan
yatra tad vijayaksetram nandiksetram ca pavanam
varāhaṁ yatra ca ksetram ye putas cakrapanina
dhatte nama vitasteti vahanti yatra jāhnavī
yatra tanmadavaksetram yatra cattaramanasam[254]

Another spot in *Kashmir, Kramasāras*, that rose from the footfall of Viṣṇu as *Trivikrama*, is hallowed by the presence of *Brahmā, Viṣṇu* and *Śiva* on a neighbouring mountain peak; and the stream that issued from the foot of *Viṣṇu* created, in *Kashmir*, another *Gaṅgā* called *Ikṣuvatī*, as if it wre another *Vitaṣṭā*:

yena Viṣṇupadenānya kasmireśu surapaga
ṣṛṣta iksuvatī nama vitaṣṭa matsarad iva [255]

This was a holy bathing place associated with all the miraculous charm that is claimed for *Gaṅgā*. A mythical spot in the

254 *Kathāsaritsāgara*, 39, 36-38.
255 *Kathāsaritsāgara,* 73, 97.

netherworld is that assigned to *Śiva* as *Hatakeśvara*, on the banks of the *Pātālagaṅgā*, the *Gaṇges* of the lower region:

> *. . . . . uttirya gaṅgām patalavahinim . . . . ayam sa devah patalanilayo hatakesvarah*[256]

It is interesting to find the term *Hatakeśvara* used for a similar deity in Indonesia and the sacred spot itself, *Hatakeśvara.* It is well known that the sacred Gaṅgā was invoked here also in some of the streams.

Gaṅgā is often conceived of as a goddess who would reveal herself now and then to heop those on whom she lowers her compassionate glance. It was therefore a regular practice to undertake tapasya not on the banks of any river or forest glade, preference being given to a bath in the *Gaṇges* and prayers on her banks. Literature teems with references to such devotional progress on the banks of the *Gaṇges*.

One particular story has it that , in despair a Brahmin swimming across the Ganges, having lost his friend, wished to put an end to his life; he prayed to the goddess *Jāhnavī, Gaṅgā*, plunging himself in the middle of the flood desiring todie. But the goddess appeared before him and gave him a charm which would render him either invisible or visible whichever he linked, aswsuring even sovereignty on earth. She disappeared only after reassuring him that he would find his friend again.

> *tavadavirabhut sākṣāt gaṅgā tasyambumadhyatah*[257]

Bones dropped in the *Gaṇges* could, just through contact with the celestial stream, transport the dead one to heaven, and this idea is often repeated in several contexts. In the well-known story of the maiden *Mandāravatī*, who was equally loved by three youths, the latter, distracted with grief on her death, attended on her remains in different ways. One gathered her bones and dropped them into

256 Ibid 73, 112-124

257 Ibid 74, 131

the *Gaṇges*. Of the other two, one used her ashes as his bed and the third, mad with grief, wanderd as a mendicant but obtained a spell that could restore her to life. The one who dropped her bones in the sacred stream was considred her son, and he who restored her to life again was almost a father to her; but the one who lay on her ashes could alone be called her husband, for he alone embraced her moral remains through his deep affection.

yascasthinī niṅayasya ganagayam sa suto matah[258]

3. Her Other Manifestations

Gaṅgā, abode of snakes

From the earliest times *Nāgas* have been associated with water, lakes, rivers, the ocean and the netherworld. There are certain *Nāgas* especially associated with *Gaṅgā*. In the *Harivaṁśa* there is mention of this type of Nāga residing in the *Gaṅgā*. It is well known from the *Mahābhārata* that *Ulupi*, the *Nāga* princess, rose from the *Gaṅgā*, her home, at the sight of *Arjuna* who stood on the river-bank and, infatuated as she was with his beauty, she pulled him down into the water in order to induce him to marry her.[259]

At *Mahābalipuraṁ*, in thelarge group of rock carvings known as *Arjuna's* penance, *Nāgas* and *Nāginis* are shown with hands clasped *Gaṅgā* on the banks of which *Arjuna* performed his *penance*. These *Nāgas* do not here represent, as they do usually, the netherworld; the diggajas do this; and as the repetition of this exposition is a blemish both in literature and in art, the snakes indicate *Gaṅgā* as the abode of the mighty Nāgas.

Again it is the *Nāgas* of the *Gaṇges* that made *Bhīma* what he was by adding prodigiously to his strength. In a garden on the banks of the *Gaṅgā*, *Duryodhana* invited his cousins for water - sport and as slumber overpowered them all at the close of the day, *Bhīma* was bound hand and foot at the instance of *Duryodhana* and dropped

258 Ibid 76, 39.

259 Dr Śivaramamurik C. op. cit. p. 85.

into the river, where, by chance he reached the abode of the *Nāgas*. Even the bite of the most venomous of the reptiles had no effect on him which instance naturally aroused their curiosity and admiration. When this came to the notice of Vāsuki, the lord of the snake world, he at once apprehended what had happened, welcomed *Bhīma* and gave him a draught of ambrosia that immediately multiplied his strength beyond all measure. So *Nāgāloka* itself is believed to be right under the *Gaṇges*, the depth of the river being unfathomable.

The tradition of the association of the *Nāgas* particularly with the Ganges continued, and when *Buddha* traveled from *Rājagṛha* to *Sṛāvasti*, having had to cross the river Gaṅgā on the way, he allowed all including the king of *Magadha* to cross the stream by boat, while he himself with his devoted pupil. *Ānanda*, crossed the river on a bridge formed by the hoods of *Nāgas* that had specially come forward to be of some help to the Enlightened One and formed this unusual bridge.[260]

The *Nāgas* are usually associated with treasures and are their guardians. It is not an unusual feature to find the container and the contained identified. Among the names of the nine well - known treatures, *śankha* and *padma* are very prominent. They also happen to be the names of snakes or *Nāgarājas*. One passage from the *Mahāvastu* is very clear on this ancient association of the *Nāgas* with *Nidhis*, and some places, with famous *Nāgas*. Like *Padma* with Ganges. The term sankha in the case of *Nāgas* such as sankhapala, *Śankha, Śankhacuda, Śankhamukha, Mahāsankha*, etc., mentioned in the texts *Mahāvastu*, *Harivaṁśa* and the *Bhāgavata* illustrate how vital the term *śankha* was. In the city of *Banaras* itself, there is an ancient well, *Nāgakuan*, *Nāgakupa*, dedicated to *Nāgarāja Ananta* or *śeṣa* where on *Nāgapancami* day, there is a special festival. Even at Allahabad, there is a temple for *Vāsuki* just overlooking the *Gaṇges* at Daraganj. *Gaṅgā's* purifying association with the snakes that considered themselves so inferior as to be sanctified even by

260 Ibid., pp. 85-86.

the touch of *Buddha's* feed on their hoods, indicates why this sacred river was chosen as their abode.

Gaṅgā, the saviour of the Vasus

Kind-hearted *Gaṅgā* alone could save the *Vasus* from the curse that was inflicted on them: that of being born on earth. As *Gaṅgā* herself had to court the similar displeasure of a sage, she took upon herself the onerous task of restoring the *Vasus* to their heavenly abode. This is why she became the glorious queen of *Śāntanu* and the progenitor of the mighty *Bhīṣma*, the *Pitāmaha* of both the *Kauravas* and the *Pāṇḍavas*. And this is why again *Bhīṣma* himself is *Gaṇgeya*. It is the intense desire of humans to associate themselves with the celestials, that explains the celestial river *Viṣṇupadī* becoming not only *Bhagīrathī*, the daughter of *Bhagīratha*, or *Haimavatī*, the daughter of *Himavan* whose roots are in the earth though the summit is at *Kailāśa*, but also the queen of an earthly monarch, *Śāntanu* himself, when she became the mother of the eight *Vasus* born on earth, including *Bhīṣma* who glorifies the progeny of *Bharata*.[261]

*Gaṅgā as mother of Sarajanm*ā

Śiva was a *Mahāyogī*, unruffled by and unyielding to Madana. But when at last for the good of the world, he discharged his retas, it was *Agni* who caught it up and unable to bear the effulgence of something so powerful, discharged it in the water of the *Gaṇges* where it collected amidst a number of reeds, *sarajala*. It is here that the child *Karttikeya* was born, six-fold, and fed by the *Kṛittikās* who had come to bathe in the *Gaṇges* and who, with maternal affection, suckled him. This baby with six heads and twelve arms was styled Kartikeya, the infant of the *Kṛttikas*; *Gangeya*, the child of *Gaṅgā*, who was, at the request of the gods, suckled by the celestial stream herself who assumed *anthropomorphic* form for the purpose.[262]

261 Ibid., p.. 87.

262 Ibid., p. 88.

taṁ payayaṁāsa sudhatipurnaṁ
surapāga svam stānam asu mūrta[263]

Agenya, the offspring of *Agni*, who was specially requested by the gods to hold the retas of *Śiva*, and *Sarajanmā* the infant born among the reeds of the *Gaṇges* where he was finally claimed by *Gaurī* herself. The birth of the warlord amidst sara or reeds which form the main part of the arrow is significant; for the birth of the child *Skanda* and the death of aged *Bhīṣma* on a bed of arrows, both sons of *Gaṅgā*, reveal that *Gaṅgā* was a *Viraṁatā*, a goddess triumphant and warlike and the parent of the highest warriorhood. The glory of *Gaṅgā*, who alone as one of the visible forms of *Śiva*, colud sustain his britghtest effulgence which exceeded even that of the sun.

raksahetor navasasibhrta vasavinam camunam
atyadityaṁ hutavahamukhe sambhrtam taddhi tejah[264]

is clearly indicated in the lines

sambhor ambumayi murtis saiva devi surapaga
tvattah smaradviso bijam durdharam dharayisyati[265]

Gaṅgā is the mother of *Skanda*. Her glory is in no small measure enhanced by this child of golden hue, born of the *Gaṇgetic* stream. It is also a symbol of the fact that gold dust is obtained from the bed of the Gaṇges and is styled *Gaṇgeya*.

Price in bringing Gaṅgā home

Lost in legend and myth is the favourite story of *Bhagīratha* who performed severe penance to please both *Brahmā* and *Śiva*, to the one to allow the flow of *Gaṅgā* and to the other to hold her for a while so that her force might not destroy the universe. But there is a greatere and more fascinating historical event of only a thousand years ago, of how *Rājendracola*, one of the greatest empersors in

263 Kumārasambhava xi, 1.
264 *Meghadūta* i, 43.
265 *Kumārasambhava* x, 26.

medieval Indian history, who greatly desired the *Gaṅgā* in his own newly established capital close to the huge temple erected by him as thanks giving for his victory to *Śiva*, brought a huge quantity of *Gaṅgā's* water from where she flows in north India to the region of the Çolas. A glance at his *Tiruvalangadu* plates amuses us when we realise that he criticized even his own ancestor *Bhagīratha* for having obtained the stream of the celestial river from Śiva through begging.

tapahprabhavadavatirnagaṅgām
Bhagīratham bahubaladdhasan sah
gaṅgājalaih pavayitum svakiyam
iyesa prthvim ravivamsadipah

That royal light of the solar race laughed at *Bhagīratha* who had *Gaṅgā* descend on earth by the intensity of his penance and decided to purify his part of the land by bringing the holy *Gaṅgā* by the might of his arm to it[266]. Of course as a devotee he bows to *Śiva*, but as a *Kṣatriya* prince, he feels that imploring *Śiva* even for *Gaṅgā* was not a proper stance. By his own might and by overcoming the rulers of the gangetic plain, the *Pālas* and the Gahadavalas, Rajendra brought the waters of the *Gaṇges* to *Gaṅgāikonḍācolapuram*. The only tribute that he asked of the defeated hosts was *Gaṇges* warter, brught by the vanquished princes in large vessels loaded on troops of elephants, all the way from thenorth to the south:

vijitais tadiyatatabhuminayakais
salilam tadiyam atha pavanam param
nijanayakaya mathurāntakāya tat
samaninayat sapadi daṅdānāyakaḥ[267]

The discovery of a *Gahayadavala* inscription in the temple of Śiva at *Gaṅgāikonḍācolapuraṁ* mentioning the Çola emperor as sovereign lord makes this event significant. The issuing of a special commemorative gold coin with the observe and reverse identical

266 South Indian Inscriptions, III, p. 400
267 South Indian Inscriptions III, p. 400.

to emphasise the importance of the bringing of the *Gaṅgā* home, by imprinting the legend *Gaṅgāikonḍācolah* in *Nagari* script, speaks volumes for the esteem in which *Gaṅgā* was held. *Rājendra* mentions the twelve mile long tank named *Colagaṅgā* that he dug in his capital ans used for holding the waters of the *Gaṅgā*, as a 'liquid pillar of victory,' *Gaṅgā jalamayajayastambha:*

> *Colagaṅgām iti khyatya prathitam nijamandale*
> *gaṅgājclamayam dhiro jayastambham vyadhatta sah*[268]

This is one of the great historical episodes in which the glory of Gaṅgā stands out most prominently.

Pride of rule over Gangetic territory

The area watered by the *Gaṇges* has always been considered the sacred land, *punyabhūmi*. In fact, this idea was so prominent in the kinds of successive kings that the *Guptas* alluded to *Gaṅgā* with pride. In an inscription of *Samudragupta's*, the rippling of *Gaṅgā* on the *jaṭās* of *Śiva* is especially mentioned, undoubtedly with pride, because the *Guptas* ruled a vast area of the plains watered by the sacred river, their own fame as immaculate as the stream. Their fame mounting higher and higher enhanced by the four expedients of appeasement, liberality, the playing off of one against another and overcoming by might speedily purifies the three worlds like the immaculate waters of the *Gaṅgā* released from their confinement in the caverns of *Paśupati's* locks:

> *pradanābhujavikramaprasamasastrarakyodayair*
> *uparyupari sancayocchritam anekamārgam yasah*
> *punati bhuvanātrayam paśupaterjatantarguha*
> *nirodhaparimoksasigrham iva pandu gaṅgām payaḥ*[269]

Normally *Rājyalakshmī*, the goddess of prosperity, sealed on a lion with feet resting on a lotus carrying the cornucopia and noose, signifying *kosā* and *danḍa* respectively, figures on the reverse

---

268 Ibid III, p. 400.

269 Corpus Inscriptionum Indikcarum III, p. 9.

of almost all of the dynasty's cions. But pride in ruling over the Gangetic area is specially indicated in the figure of the river goddess on her *Makara* shown on the reverse of some coins such as the tiger slayer type of *Samudragupta's* time and the *Khadgatrata* type of Kumaragupta. As in the case of the figure of Devāsena fondling the peacock, the mount of her warlord, whose army she personalifies, and which theme indirectly suggests *Kumāragupta*, the king himself, with his army as powerful as that of the celestials', devasend, Gaṅgā on the reverse of the coins here suggests how pure and apotless was the fame of the Gupta kings and how wonderfully watered by the sacred stream was their vast and prosperous empire, stretching from Punjab to Assam. Incidentally, the *rhino-hunt* type of coin is indicative of the home of the rhino, Assam, that came under the rule of the Guptas, *Gaṅgā* on *Makara* in these Gupta coins is again a unique feature, and a glorification of the sacred river, association with whom, through their territory, the Guptas greatly prided.

Inspiration of Gaṅgā in islands beyond the seas

The spirit of Gaṅgā whorship traveled with the pious Hindu wherever he went, and it is no wonder that in far-off *Indonesia* in central *Java*, an inscription on a huge boulder near the well-known spring called *Tuk Mas*, 'the Golden Spring' near the volcano *Merbabu* is a verse inn *Pallava* Grantha characters of about the fifth century A.D., glorifying the spring as being nearly as sacred as the holy river *Gaṅgā* herself:

> *.... usucyamburuhanujatā*
> *kvacicchilavalukanirgaeyaṁ*
> *kvacitprakirna subhasitatoya*
> *samprasrta medhyakariva gaṅgā.*

'(Here) flows forth (the streamlet) purifying as the ganges, arising out of the bright (?) lotus . . . . at some places gushing out of the sand and stones, and at others widening its limpid and cool waters.'

Dr. B.C. Chhabra's query as to whether the first line refers to *Viṣṇu's* lotus feet from which Gaṅgā sprang and to which this spring is likened, is answered in the affirmative. In *Campa*, the My-son stele inscription dated A.D. 657 mentions a *Gaṅgāraja* who renounced the throne to take to a life on the banks of the *Jāhnavī* or *Gaṇges*:[270]

prayad to jahnavim

In east *Java*, the famous carving of *Viṣṇu* on *Garuḍa* representing Erlanga has carved on the walls of a monument in its vicinity, river goddesses with their nipples spurting jets of water in the beautifylly conceived and constructed fountain. This idea of water oozing from the breast follows from the line:

> *yo hemakumbhastananissṛtanāṁ*
> *skandasya matuh payasaṁ rasajnah*[271]

It is the taste of the water issung from the pitcher-like breasts of the mother of *Skanda*. The mother of *Skanda* could be either *Pārvatī* or *Gaṅgā*, but in this case, the appropriateness of the image is inclined towards *Gaṅgā*. Actually, *Gaṅgā* holding a water vessel, as she should be depicted according to the iconographic text of the *Viṣṇudharmotara*, allows the jet to issue forth from her breast. It is the appreciation and perpetuation of this concept of *Gaṅgā* in eleventh century *Java* that should especially arrest our attention.

The greatness of *Gaṅgā* is not easily recounted. Sight of her purifies, bathing in here waters frees one from sin, the utterance of her name transports one by a magic ladder, as it were, to the highest heaven. The Indian sculptor has not in the least lagged behind the bard, who has sung the glories of this great river, in presenting her in all her glorious aspects. Like *Vālmikī* who describes *Puṣpaka* and, not being fully satisfied, goes again and again into ecstasies over it, *Kālidāsa* excels himself in his description of *Gaṅgā*

---

270 Dr Chhabra, B.C., Expansion of Indo Aryan culture during Pallava rule, Delhi 1965 (As evinced by inscriptions)

271 *Raghuvaṁśa* it, 36.

wherever opportunity occurs and especially in the tenth canto of the *Kumārasambhara*. In his own words let us put the same question:

kam nabhinandayatyesa drṣṭa piyusavāhinī[272]

The earlier Vedic literature does not describe Varuṇa as a concrete figure. But later, when image worship came into vogue, there are directions for sculptured images of *Varuṇa*. The *Bṛhatsaṁhitā* says that *Varuṇa* should be made slightly pot-bellied, seated on a chariot drawn by seven swans, a four-armed figure holding the lotus, the noose, the conch-shell and a jewelbox with his consort *Gaurī* on his lap. *Gaṅgā* and *Yamunā* should accompany the group. In the *Rājarānī* temple in *Bhubaneswar* (Orissa) there is an actual image of *Varuṇa*, where he is two-armed, and seated on a makara (a mythical sea-animal or a crocodile). From the *Bṛhatsamhitā* description certain important features of the concept of *Varuṇa* emerge. His pot-belly indicates his association with the *Śiva*-group in which many popular non-Aryan gods were assimilated. *Kuvera* the god of wealth is pot bellied; so is the popular *Śiva* of certain regions, so also is *Gaṅeśa* and the *Agni* committing adultery with the six sages wives, and it is the nucleus of the story of *Skanda's* birth. *Śiva's* holding the Gaṅgā on his head and *Agni* depositing his seed in the river brings them closere. All the gods of this group have ape-sons; *Varuṇa* (*Hemakuta* and *Ṛṣabha*), *Yama* (*Sumukha* and *Durmukha*), Vayu (Hanumat), *Śiva* has an ape-shaped associate of Nandin, Vanararupa, ape-shaped. *Agni* alsohas ape-sons, *Nila*[273]*Agni* hid from the gods and entered the earth in the shape of a mole.[274]

The mole is offered to *Śiva* in the *Satarudrīya* as Śiva's share and in later mythology it became Ganesa's mount. Thus *Agni's* assuming that particular shape associates him with *Śiva* and *Gaṇeśa*. Of the seven mothers of *Agni* recorded in the Mahābhārata. one is Rudra, a feminine form of *Rudra*. But the fact that brings *Agni* and *Rudra*

272 Kumārasambhava x, 48.

273 Rām. IV: 41: 3, V: I: 47) and Samādhāna (Rām VI: 3: 25).

274 TB I : I : 3 : 3.

closest to each other is the ambiguous parenthood of *Kārttikeya*, who is called the son of *Śiva* and *Agni* in different accounts. The intent seems to have been to say that *Śiva* in his *Agni* form begot *Kārttikeya. Agni* at one time cast his eyes on the waters... the seed became gold, for this reason the latter shines like fire.[275] Gold sprang from *Agni's* seed.[276] The AV (Atharva-Veda) reports that the waters hid the gold (AV XIX : 27 : 9) and this seems to form the real nucleus of the story of Skanda;s birth.

Agni is called *Sahasramuṣka* (with a thousand scrota) this reminds us of the emphasis on the virility of *Śiva*, of his *Urdhvalinga* or *Mahasepha* image and perhaps indirectly associates Agni with the phallic cult. *Agni* desires heaven should offer the Agnistoma sacrifice, for by it one conquers *Yama's* region.[277] The *Purāṇas* lay it down that for wealth *Agni* should be approached. In the *Agnicayana* ceremony, some hairs should be cut from the goat and mixed with clay, while the offerer says, 'I mix thee, herein, the well-born *Jaṭāvedas*. The goat is thus a symbol of *Agni* ; it is also the mount of *Puṣaṇ*, another god of this group. *Atatayin* (with a drawn bow); he is frequently called *Bhīma* (mighty). The *Vedic Rudra* carries how and arrows, the bow is golden and kills byh the thousand[278]. His cruelty is referred to in the TS nucleus of the *Tṛipuradahana* episode. AJB narrative says: the gods decided to leave behind whetever was crued in them; they put the dross on potsherds: in it was born this god. Because he was born on *Saravas* (potsherds) he is thus called (*Sarva*).[279] This again mentions *Śiva's* cruelty. Of *Śiva's* other feats the most significant and important is his holding the *Gaṅgā* on his head. The Vedic literature contains no reference to it, perhaps because the *Gaṅgā* did not attain its sanctity in that period and the holiness of the pilgrimages strewn on the banks on this river had not

---

275 SB II : I : I : 5.

276 SB III : 9 : 4 : I.

277 MU VI : 36.

278 AV XI : 2 : 12.

279 JB m: 26 : 2.

been so established and recognized a fact as in the *epic-Purāṇic* age. Thus its first mention is found in the epics.

The *Rāmāyaṇa* giving the story says that *Śiva* agreed to hold the descending *Gaṅgā* on his head.[280] The descent is described in vivid language. *Gaṅgā*, it is significant to note, is the elder sister to *Umā* (I:37:16-19). *Brahmā* instructed *Bhagīratha* about *Gaṅgā's* descent and also tells him that *Śiva* alone could hold the tumult of the descending torrent. Arriving on the earth, she becomes *Bhagīratha's* daughter and is called *Bhāgirathī*[281] and *Bhagīratha* praises her. In the Mbh, the river asks *Bhagīratha* ot beg *Śiva* to hold her (III: 107:8, 9). He does so, *Śiva* agrees, and is called *Jāhnāvidhrk* (XIII:13:137). The 60,000 sons of *Sagara* who lay burnt to ashes are saved through the contact of the river. The episode clearly has one purpose: to emphasize the power and sanctity of *Śiva*. Incidentally it appears as essentially bound up with the *epic-Puranic* religion, which has idol-worship, temples, vows and pilgrimages with all of which the rising *Śiva* cult is connected. *Śiva-culture* flourished along the banks of the *Gaṅgā*. *Varanasi* is on its bank and *Śiva* is called *Kāśinātha*, which is probably a reminiscence of a local *Śaiva* cult with its central shrine in *Varanasi*. The addition of the story of the purging of the ashes in the place now called *Sagara* (i.e. the Bay of Bengal, south of Bengal) indicates the south-eastern course of the *Aryan* peoples' progress; it also includeds all the region along the banks of the river. From *Kailāśa*, the epic home of Śiva, via *Varanasi*, *Prayāga* (Allahabad) down to the Bay of Bengal the entire course of the river is included in thetract over which Saivism spread and flourished.

It is evident in present-day India *Śiva* is more frequently worshipped in his phallic form than in the iconic. Pebbles smoothed by the *Narmadā* are called Bānalinga, phallic emblems of Śiva. The cult is traced to the ṚV where the Vedic *Aryan* swears at the 'barbarians' describing them as *Śiśnadevas* (people to whom the *phallus* is a god). According to *Nirukta* IV: 19 the word means *lustful*. Thus the exact

280 Ram I : 37:20-I.

281 Ram I:45 : 56.

import of the word is far from certain. Nor is it certain whether there were actual *phallus* - worshippers among the non-Vedic population; but this seems a probable assumption, for in *Mohenjo-Daro* and Harappa plenty of clay and stone representations of the male organ are found. Vedic literature is silent about *phallic* worship and seems to adjure and curse it in a few passages. It is in the epics that we hear of it for the first time. The *Rām*, mentions *Rāvaṇa's* worship of *Rudra* in the *phallic* (*linga*) form.[282] By the time the Mbh. assumed its present form, *phallic* worship was an established mode of *Śiva* worship. This we hear that sages and gods have always worshipped the erect phallus[283] and that linga worship is an alternative form of image worship. The *Uṣaṇas* episode emphasizes the significance of the *phallus*. Upamanyu declining the boon offered by *Indra* said *Śiva* was his god because creation was not marked by a lotus (*Laksmī's* symbol) or a disc (*Viṣṇu's*) or a thunderbolt (*Indra's*), but by the male and female organs which proves that *Śiva* and *Pārvatī*; are the supreme deities, and that creation belonged to them.[284] Once *Pitāmaha Bhahman* commissioned *Śiva* for creation. *Śiva* dived under water to meditate. *Brahman*, impatient at the delay, appointd another who accomplished creation. When *Śiva* emerged from under water and saw that another had performed his task he grew furious in indignation, plucked his own procreative organ as superfluous now and planted it on theearth. He told Brahman that through meditation he had procured food for the future creation first, hence the delay.

Gaṅgā is a divine origin. She is originated from *Kamanḍalu* of *Brahmā* via *Jaṭā* of Lord *Śiva*. From *Śiva's Jaṭā*. She desmids to the Earth.

282 VII:31:42-3, also KP XXI: 48.

283 Mbh. VII : 200 : 92-6, VII : 201 : 124 - 5.

284 Mbh. XIII : 144 : 33.

SELECT BIBLIOGRAPHY

A. SOURCE MATERIAL

Aeschylus. Agarnemnon (Loeb edn.). E'.tmenides (Loeb edo.), Prometheus Bound (Loeb edn.). The Libation Bearers (Loeb edn.).

Agnipurāṇa (Anaridasrama Sanskrit series no. 45).

Aiteraya Brahmana (ed. A. K. Shastri, Travancore, 1942).

Apastamba Dharmasāstra (Bombay Sanskrit series, 1932).

Apastamba Grhysütra (ed. C. Shastri, Chowkhaeuba Sanskrit series, 1928; also Vienna, 1887).

Ahastamba, rautasütra (Baroda Oriental Institute, 1955).

Apollodorus: Bibliotheca (Loeb edn.).

Apuleius: The Golden Ass (Loeb edo.).

Aivalayana Grhyasaltra (ed. P. Shastri, Poona, 1936).

Atvalayana Srautasutra (Anandasrama series, 1913)

Atharvaved.a Sagshitā (Svadhyayamandala series, Bombay).

Atharvaveda Saṅhita (Harvard Oriental series).

Avesta (ed. J. Darmesteter, Sacred Books of the East Series).

Baudhdyāna Dharmasāstra (Chowkhamba Sanskrit series, 1934)

Baudhayāna Srauta Sutra (ed. Caland, Bibliotneca Indica, 'o7),

Bhavisya Purāṇa (Gita Press, Gorokhpur).

Chandogya Brahmana (Sanskrit College Research Series, 1958).

Egyptian Book of the Dead, The (Kegan Paul, 1905).

Euripides Bacchae (Loeb edn.).

Hippolytus (Loeb edn.).
Iphigenia in Tauris (Loeb edn.).
The Libation Bearers (Loeb edn.).
Garuḍia Purāṇa (ed. M. N. Datta, Calcutta, 1908).
Gautama Dharmasütra (ed. G. Buhler, Bombay, 1892).
Gilgarnesh, The Epic of (Eng. tr. by 'N. K. Sanders, Penguin, 1960).
Gobhila Ghya Sütra (Calcutta, 1936).
Gopatha Brahmana (E. J. Brill, Leyden).
Harivaṁśa (Calcutta, 1839).
Herodotus: The Histories (Londdon.).
Hesiod: Theogony (Loeb edn.).
Homer: The Iliad (Loeb edn.).
The Ho1y Bible (Authorized Version).
The Odyssey (Loeb edo.). Also Oxford University Press, New York, 1946.
Tiddi Upani, cads (The Upanitads, Nirnayasagar Press 1946; also ix Upaniṣads, Bibi. nd. 1935).
Jaiminiya Brahmana (Nagpur International Academy of Indian Culture, 1954).
Kausitaki Brahmana (Bibliotheca Indica, 1865).
Kurma Purāṇa (Calcutta, 1926).
Przvluski, J.: Varuna god of sea and sky (JRAS, 1931).
The great Goddess in India and Iran (Ind. Hist. Quart. 1934).
Renou, L.: Sur Ia notion de Brahman (J. Asiatique, 1949).
Ronnow, K.: Viivarupa (Rahson Comm. Vol. 1930-2).
Sur, A. K.: Pre-Aryan elements in Indian culture (md. Hist. Quart. 1934.
Thieme, P.: The Aryan gods of the Mitanni treaties (J,-IOS, vol. 80, no. 4, 1960),
Thomas, F. W.: The expansion of Indianism (Oriental Congress, 1937),
Vader, V. H.: Twin gods Atvinau (md. Hist. Quart. 1932).
Wesendonk, O. G. von: The Kslavkda and the Zervanite system (JRAS, 593!).
Winternitz, M.: Race and religion (Prabuddha Bharata, Aug.).
Zimmerman, H.: God in the Gathas and in the RV. (JCOI, 1932).

B. DICTIONARIES AND ENCYCLOPAEDIAS

Real-encyclopaedia der klessischcn Altertumstvissenschaft (A. Pauly and G. Wissowa).
The New Schaff - Herzog encyclopaedia of religious knowledge (Michigan, 1958).

Hastings' encyclopaedia of religion and ethics (1958).

International bibliography of the historyt of religions (ed. C.J.Blecker, Leiden).

Larousse encyclopaedia of mythology (London, 1954).

Standard dictionary of folk-lore, mythology and legend (Leach and Fried, 1949-50).

Motiv-index in folk-lore literature (ed. S. Thompson, Indiana).

Concise encyclopaedia of living faiths (R.C.Zaehner, Hutchison, 1959).

Oxford classical dictionary (Clarendon Press, Oxford).

Sanskrit - English dictionary (M. Monier-Williams, Clarendon Press, Oxford).

The encyclopaedia of myths and legends of all nations (H.S. Robinson and K. Wilson, London, 1962).

Civilisation past and present (ed. T.W. Walbank and A.M. Taylor, Chicago, 1949).

C. DICTIONARIES AND ENCYCLOPAEDIAS

Abbott, J. 1932. The keys of power: a study of Indian reitual and belief. London. Methuen and Co.

Aitchison, Jean. 1987, Words in themind: an introduction to the mental lexicon. Oxford: Basil Black wall Ltd.

Aiyangar, B.N. 1913. 'Funeral ceremonies'. Quarterly Journal of the Mythic Society, 4:13-25.

Aiyar, K.V. Rangaswami, 1941. Introduction to Krtyakalpataru of Bhatta Laksmidhara, vol. 5, Danakhanda. Baroda: Gaekwad's Oriental Series 91.

Alexander, J. and P. Alexander. 1987. 'Striking a bargain in Javanese markets', Man (n.s.) 22, 1:42-68.

All about Benares, 1918. Benares: K.S. Muthiah and Co.

Altekar, A.S. 1947, Benares and Sarnath: past and present. Varanasi: Banaras Hindu University.

Amrit Suniol, Unruly river waters - How mountain rivers and monsoons have stopped South Asian History, New Delhi, 2018.

Arnold, David. 1989. 'The ecology and cosmology of disease in the Banaras region'. In S.B. Freitag (ed.) Culture and power in Banaras: community. performance and environment, 1800 - 1980: 246-67. Berkeley: University of California Press.

Babb, L.A. 1975. The Divine Hierarchy: Popular Hinduism in Central India. New York: Columbia University Press.

Bakker, Hans. 1984, Ayodhya: the history of Ayodhya from the 7th century B.C. to the middle of the 18th century, its development into a sacred centre with special reference to the 'Ayodhyamahātmya and to the worship of Rama according to the 'Agastyasaṁhitā', Groningen: University of Groningen.

Balfour, H. 1897, 'The life-hostory of an Aghori fakir'. Journal of the Anthropological Institute (London), 26:340-57.

Barrow, H.W. 1893, 'On Aghoris and Aghoripanthis' Journal of the Anthropological Society of Bombay, 3: 197-251.

Bayly, C.A. 1981, 'From ritual to ceremony: death ritual and society in Hindu north India since 1600'. In Joachim Whaley (ed.), Mirrors of mortality: studies in the social history of death: 154-86. London : Europa Publications Ltd. 1983. Rulers, townsmen and bazaars: north Indian society in theage of British expansion, 1770 - 1870. Cambridge: Cambridge University Press.

Beck, B.E.F. 1976. 'The symbolic merger of body, space and cosmos in Hindu Tamil Nadu'. Contrib utions to Indian Sociology (n.a.), 10, 2:213-43.

Beliappa, J. and M. Kaushik. n.d. 'The food of well - being'. Paper prepared for the ACLS-SSRC Joint Committee on South Asia (Sub-committee on South Asian).

Bhattacharya Sukumar The Indian Theogony, Penguin, India Calcutta, 2000)

Dasgupta Surendra Nath. A history of Indian Philosophy Vol. V. Southeren school of Saivism Cambridge 1932, Delhi (Reprint), 1975-1988.

Gonda J. Aspects of early Viṣṇuism, Delhi, 1969.

Giri, Kapildep (ed) Gaṅgāvatarana of Nilkantha Dikshit, Varanasi, 1985.

Mukhopadhyaya Durga Prasad, Gaṅgā bhakti Tarangini, Calcutta, 1885.

Narayana R.K. God, Demans and others, 1993.

Pandey, Kanti Chandra (Gen. editor) R.C. Dwivedi An outline of History of Saiva Philosophy.

Parry, Jaganatham, Death in Banaras, New Delhi, 1944.

Pt. Jagarnath Gaṅgālahari (The flow of ganges) Varanasi, 2007.

Pt. Kedarnath Sastri (ed), The Gaṅgā Vataraṇa of Nilkantha Dikshit, Bombay 1916.

Ramanujan, Speaking of Shiva (Three hundred Rāmāyaṇas five examples and three thoughts on Translation Berkeley, 1991.

Sen, Sudipta, Gaṅgā, The way pasts of a river, Gurgaon, 2019.

Wilson, G. 1939. 'Nyakusa conventions of burial. Bantu Studies, 13:1-31.

Wilson, P.J. 1967. Status ambiguity and spirit possession. Man (n.s.), 2, 3:366-78.

Wirth, Louis. 1975 (1938). 'Urbanism as a way of life'. In John Friedl and Loel J. Chrisman (eds), City ways: a selective reader in urban anthropology: 26-45. New York: Thomas Y. Crowell.

Wiser, W.H. 1936. The Hindu jajmani system, Lucknow: Lucknow Publishing House, Wittgenstein. L. 1958. Philosophical investigations (trans. G.E.M. Anscombe). Oxford: Basil Blackwell

Yang, Anand. 1987. 'The many faces of sati in theearly nineteenth century'. Manushi 1987:26-9.

Zehner, R.C. 1962. Hinduism. London: Oxford University Press.

INDEX

I

J

K

T

U

V

W

Y

Z

1. *Brahmā* pouring water on Viṣṇu's food, *Hoysala*, 12th century A.D., *Nuggihajji*, Mysore.

2. *Brahmā* pouring water on Viṣṇu's foot, Western Çālukya, 12th century A.D., *Hampi*, Mysore.

3. Umāsaṃhitā Śiva receiving Gaṅgā on his locks, approaching in *Gaṅgāvataraṇa*, karana, 10th century A.D., Nepal.

4. *Gaṅgādhara*, close-up, suggesting the receiving of Gaṅgā on his locks by Śiva. Early Çola, 9th century A.D. Koyumbatur, Tamil Nadu.

5. Gaṅgā as *cāmaradhāriṅī*, along with *Gauri*, for *Naṭarāja* dancing on *bull*. *Pāla*, 11th century A.D. *Śankarbandha*, Bangladesh.

6. *Gaṅgā* approaching Śiva as a bride, *Gupta*, 5th century A.D., *Rajouna*, Bihar.

7. *Gaṅgādhara* appeasing *Pārvatī*, while receiving Gaṅgā on his locks. Early *Çola*, 11th century A.D. *Gaṅgāikoṇḍācolapuram*, Tamil Nadu.

8. *Gaṅgādhara* with *Pārvatī* vexed with her face turned away. Early *Çola*, 11th century A.D. *Mayuram*, Tamil Nadu.

9. *Gaṅgā* as an umbrella or *caurī* or canopy above *Śiva*, *Pallava*, 7th century A.D. *Kāncīpuram*, Tamil Nadu, National Museum.

10. *Gaṅgā* with a stream as her lower part, late Cola, 12th century A.D., *Darasuram*, Tamil Nadu.

11. *Naṭarāja* with Gaṅgā on his *jaṭās*. Early Çola, 11th century A.D., Art Gallery, Tanjavur, Tamil Nadu.

12. Wavy pattern of *jaṭās* for *Naṭarāja*, late *Çola*, 12th century A.D.

13. *Gaṅgā*, compassionate, and purifier of thought, beside *Daksiṇāmūrti*, *Gupta*, 5th century A.D., *Ahicchatra*, Uttar Pradesh.

14. *Bhīṣma* on bed of arrows surrounded by sages sent by *Gaṅgā*, *Pāṇḍavas* and Kṛṣṇa, Kisangarh school, 18th century A.D., Bharat Kala Bhavan Museum, Banaras.

15. *Bhiṣma* on *śaratalpa* or bed of arrows surrounded by sages, some in the guise of *haṁsas* (geese), *Kauravas*, *Panḍavas*, and *Arjuna* and *Kṛṣṇa*, in a *chariot*. Early Western Çālukya, 8th century A.D. *Paṭṭadakal*, Karnataka.

16. *Gaṅgā* as *Nadimatrkā* on either side of *Nāgarāja* Mucalinda, *Sātavāhana*, 2nd century A.D., *Amarāvatī*, Andhra Pradesh.

17 & 18. Goddess carrying food and water, *Nādīmātṛka*, Kuśāṇa, 2nd century A.D., Bharat Kala Bhavan, Varanasi, Uttar Pradesh.

19. Goddess carrying food and water, Nādimatṛka, Kuśāṇa, 2nd century A.D., Mathura Museum, Uttar Pradesh.

20. *Purṇakumbha* representing *Gaṅgā* and *Yamunā* flanking the doorway. Early Western *Çālukya*, 6th century A.D., *Aihole*, Mysore.

21. *Gaṅgā* as guardian of gateway on doorjamb. *Vijayanagara*, 16th century A.D. *Hampi*, Mysore

22. Terracottas, the largest of the kind, representing *Gaṅgā* and *Yamunā* as guardians of the gateway of *Śiva*, *Ahicchatra*, Uttar Pradesh.

23. *Gaṅgā* and *Yamunā* as guardians of gateway of *Śiva*, *Gupta*, 5th century A.D., *Dah Pārvatīya*, Assam.

24. Close up of *Gaṅgā* and *Yamunā* as guardians of the gateway of *Śiva, Gupta*, 5th century A.D., *Dah Pārvatīya*, Assam.

25. *Gaṅgā* on her *Makara* with attendants as guardians of the doorway. *Gurjara Pratihāra*, Gwalior, Madhya Pradesh.

26. The confluence of the three rivers, *Triveni sangama, Gupta,* 4th century A.D., *Udayagiri*, Madhya Pradesh.

27. *Gaṅgā* as *Suranimnaga* or heavenly stream under the *Kalpa tree*. Sena, 12th century A.D., Mahanad, West Bengal.

28. *Gaṅgāvisarjanamūrti*, *Raṣṭrakūṭa*,
8th century A.D. Ellora.

29. *Gaṅgā* received in the water vessel of sage *Jāhnu* and released again through his ear to flow from the *Himalaya*. Western *Çālukya*, 8th century A.D., *Paṭṭadakal*, Mysore.

30. *Gaṅgādhara* receiving *Gaṅgā* as a triple stream, *Tṛipathaga Tṛisortas*, *Vakataka*, 5th century A.D., *Elephanṭā*, Maharashtra.

31. *Gaṅgā* flowing onto *Śiva's* locks and released therefrom by the prayers of *Bhagīratha*, Western *Çālukya*, 8th century A.D. *Paṭṭadakal*, Mysore.

32. *Gaṅgādhara* with one foot placed on ignorance represented by a dwarf, and receiving the pure and enlightening *Gaṅgā*. *Pallava*, 7th century A.D., Tiruchirapalli, Tamil Nadu.

33. Penance and nityakarmanusthāna - snāna, *suryopasthana*, *dingnamaskara*, Vasodaka, etc. *Pallava*, 7th century A.D., *Mahabalīpuram*, Tamil Nadu.

34. The three streams, *Sarasvatī*, *Gaṅgā* and Yamunā, Raṣṭrakuṭa, 8th century A.D., Ellora.

35. Commemorative Gold Coin of *Rajendra Çola*, Çola tiger flanked by Cera bow and *Pāṇḍya* fish with legend on observe and reverse in *Nagari*: *Gaṅgāikoṇḍā Colah,* 11th century A.D., National Museum.

36. Khaḍga Gold Coin of *Kumāragupta*, observe : King on horse fighting rhinoceros and legend bharta *Khadgatrata* Kumaragupta Jayatyanisam; reverse: *Gaṅgā* standing on Makara, umbrella held over her and legend *Sri Mahendra Khaḍga*, National Museum.

37. River goddess with jets of water issuing from *purṇakumbha* breasts as from a fountain, Sailendra, 11th century A.D., *Belahan*, East Java.

38. *Gaṅgā* in Aqueous Form *KĀSĪ*
(*Dasasvamedhaghāṭa* - Banaras)

. 39. *Gaṅgā* at the Burning Ghāṭ (Cremation) *KĀSĪ* (*Maṇikaraṇikā Ghāṭ*)

40. *Gaṅgā's Gomukh Glacier* (Pilgrim Trail Toward Gomukh)

41. *Gaṅgādhara* - (Lord *Śiva* with *Gaṅgā*)

42. *Gaṅgā* and *Yamunā* - Terracotta Images - *Ahichhatra*

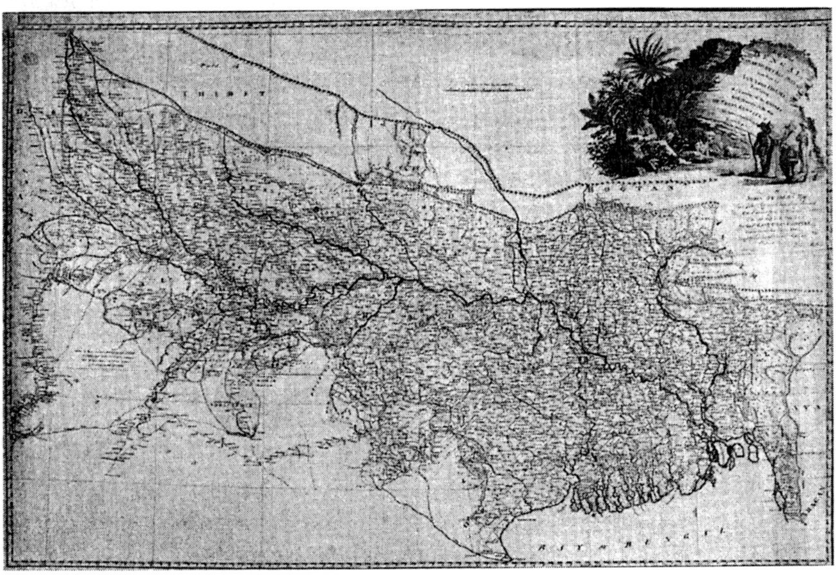

43. *Gaṅgā* (Aqueous form) in Map of Bengal, Bihar, Awadh and Allahabad exhibiting the course of the *Gaṇges* From *Hardwar* to the Sea (1786).

44. *Śiva* Bearing the Descent of the *Gaṅgā* River Painting - Himachal Pardesh C. 1740.